Praying in the Power Zone

Elevate Your Frequency, Quiet Your Mind, and

Enhance Your Prayers with Pure Essential Oils

To Tom & Kim,
Thank you for all you do
& who you are.
Be blessed ~
Janine

Janine Logue Wooten

Mandala Gallery Publishing

2017

If you would like to know which oils I personally love and use with these prayers please request the free companion guide to this book. You can find me on FB at "Praying in the Power Zone."

DEDICATION

This book is dedicated to you the reader; you who love God and seek a deeper connection with the Divine, you who share the vision of a better world, where all are living vibrant, purposeful, abundant lives, you who care enough to make an effort to improve your lives. May you be richly blessed by this offering.

PRAYING IN THE POWER ZONE

"Prayer can work without oils. Oils can work without prayer. When both are used together, each increases the power of the other such that their combined ability to heal is greater than the sum of the two. This is no coincidence. It was programmed into the oils by God from their creation. Prayer and oils were meant to be used together."

—David Stewart PhD, Healing Oils of the Bible

"When I hear something ancient that matches cutting edge science—I perk up—I stop what I am doing—I want to find out more. Because something simple like this—often changes your life forever."

—FreeNeville.com

Heartfelt Prayer + Pure Essential Oils = Prayer in the Power Zone

—Janine Logue Wooten

TABLE OF CONTENTS

Breaking Free

INTRODUCTION

"... And the leaves of the trees were for the healing of the nations."
—Revelations 22:2

If you're like me, you always try to do your best, and you want to live a life that honors God. You pray often, but sometimes you feel like the prayers, or the energy in them just falls flat. While you know intellectually that God hears your prayers, you long for that heartfelt connection—to feel more connected on a deeper level emotionally and spiritually.

More often than not, we are too busy, too exhausted, or just pulled in too many directions. The result is that our prayers get interrupted with distractions, both from the external world around us, and by our own incessant internal chatter.

Having on occasion experienced being fully present with God—being still, quiet, and feeling totally connected during your prayer time—you know how truly amazing that can be. And you would love to have that experience during your prayer time more often. Being able to feel that level of focus and connection with our Creator, our Loving Father, by definition should be an "AWE-some" experience!

This book is meant as a resource to that end. It explores one very effective and perhaps little known method to help bridge the gap: the use of pure essential oils as an effective enhancement to our prayers.

Studies have shown, and we know by our own experience, that prayer can be very effective, in and of itself. Introducing pure essential oils into our prayer time is a wonderful way to get our hearts and minds into a more connected space for communicating with God.

This book came about from countless books read, endless hours of study, and the inevitable compilation of my own life experiences. I wanted to gather information from several different excellent sources, and make it available in one place, easy to use and understand.

The purpose for this book is twofold: to help you understand how wonderful and effective pure essential oils can be, and to show you one way to experience a more profound prayer life. I pray that it will bless you and that you will find value in it, whether you are just starting to learn about essential oils, or you are a seasoned veteran of the "oily lifestyle."

Prayer and pure essential oils go hand in hand for anyone wanting to experience a more focused prayer time, elevate their own frequency, improve their life, live more "on purpose," and leave a positive impact on their world.

Pure essential oils can be thought of as the "life essence" of the plant, and each plant has its own personality, so to speak. Part of any plant's individual profile is a certain energetic frequency. Therefore, when we apply or inhale the essence of a particular plant (i.e., the essential oil of a plant), we are partaking of this frequency. This can have the effect of raising our own frequency, and literally putting our thoughts—and our prayers!—closer to God energetically.

This book is a resource as to one way that anyone can begin to use pure essential oils, and to see and feel the benefit right away. It is very simple, easy to implement, and effective, so even if you're new to essential oils, you won't feel lost or overwhelmed by not knowing where to start. You can start experiencing them in a wonderful way, right away!

Additionally, if you know of someone who you would like to introduce to the essential oils lifestyle, this might be a nice, easy introduction to that person. What a great way to say, "I care about you!"

God's word shows us that He intends that we use the plants for our well-being! What a beautiful way to start our essential oil journey— using the oils in combination with prayer and with gratitude!

However, it is not necessary to be an essential oil enthusiast to find value in the prayers. Many have enjoyed these prayers and found them beneficial on their own.

This book is for you if you want to enhance your prayer life, if you want to feel more connected and present with God, or if you want to understand more about using pure essential oils for well-being.

If you pray (whether or not you use pure essential oils), if you want to feel closer to God, or you want to experience a more peaceful and natural state of well-being, you have found the right place!

"There is treasure to be desired and oil in the dwelling of the wise ..."
—Proverbs 21:20

"Pray without ceasing."

—1 Thessalonians 5:1

PERSONAL NOTE
FROM THE AUTHOR

It will be helpful to have a basic understanding of how essential oils can enhance your prayer time before we get into the specific prayers. In Part One we will briefly cover exactly that, to give you a foundation of understanding, thus strengthening your belief. You might be tempted to skip this section, however it's important to understand how and why this works, because I believe that part of the difference in results is largely due to the following factors:

Belief, Intent, Energy, and Purity.

That being said, you do not need to "believe" in essential oils for them to be effective in your body. However, having faith and applying them intentionally makes a positive difference, in my opinion. Understanding the science and using oils with faith results in both elements working together for the most effective results.

In *Science and Religion—Toward the Restoration of an Ancient Harmony*, Anjam Khursheed states that if science is true, and religion is true, then the two must necessarily agree. If there is disharmony in their tenets, we must conclude that we do not yet know all there is to know, meaning the problem is due to the limits of our human understanding, and not with the truths themselves. He likens this to trying to learn how a computer processor works, but only being able to see bits and pieces at a time, as if looking through a pegboard. In other words, we don't have all the puzzle pieces—we can't yet see the entire picture.

The reason I bring this up is that it tells my story in a way. In my early years, my mom was always more faith based, and my dad (a doctor), more scientific. This left me trying to reconcile the two. I've spent a lifetime studying both sides of the equation and looking for that place where truth meets truth. This is one reason I am so fascinated with the study of essential oils!

It is so exciting being alive at this time, as we are actually able to watch as the divide narrows between the two. Science is changing as it grows, with the theory of relativity, chaos theory and quantum physics rapidly moving more into the realms of energy work, creative visualization, and conscious acts of creation. I believe this to be the same energy that explains faith, creation, prayer and miracles.

Whereas in the past it was believed that one had to choose between two very opposing belief systems, we are now witnessing the two systems find common ground in the realms of frequency, consciousness, and intention. The new paradigm brings with it new language that both the faith-based and the more scientific minded can understand, and even begin to agree upon.

The once impossible leap from one to the other is now but a small—even inevitable—step. Truth is truth, and the more we know, the more the two are beginning to agree. Of course they do! It cannot be any other way!

Essential oils provide the scientific part of the equation, and the prayers provide the faith-based part of the equation. The results are synergistic, with the combined affect being greater than the sum of the individual parts. This is where "awesome" happens! This is what I call enhanced prayer, or praying in the power zone!

Pure Essential Oils + Heart Centered Prayer = AMAZING Results!

My prayer is that you are blessed by what you will learn in the following pages. Please share your experiences adding pure essential oils to your prayer time by visiting the Facebook Group "Praying in the Power Zone with Pure Essential Oils." I would love to see this group grow into a place where everyone can share answered prayers and help one another grow in faith.

An Overview of the Structure of the Book

Part I is a quick look at how and why pure essential oils "work." We very briefly touch on just a few of the factors that support using essential oils as an enhancement to our natural wellness. The goal is to give you a basis for understanding and leave you with a desire for further independent study.

Part II is a collection of prayers, categorized by themes based on various needs you might have at different times in your life. There are many wonderful pure essential oils and oil blends that can be effectively used with each of these prayers. In Part V, you will find a few examples of properties of essential oils that you can use as a starting point when pairing oils with particular prayers.

Part III is a collection of prayers specifically for anyone interested in blessing their business. I noticed when compiling the prayers that several addressed my growing team of business partners. For your convenience, I am duplicating those prayers in a section specific to that purpose. There are twenty-one, so you can plan a three-week prayer blast over your business and watch what happens. God is faithful!

Part IV explains why purity is of utmost importance and how to know if an essential oil is truly pure. If you use essential oils (or are just beginning to learn), you need to know this information.

Part V offers further foundational information. It's especially important that you read the first two sections: "The Basics of Using Essential Oils" and "What To Do and What Not To Do." There is also a section that demonstrates an example of how you might research the many beneficial properties of essential oils.

My intention is that this book be a valuable resource that you can use anytime you have a need, by finding prayers that will be helpful, and by knowing which essential oils and oil blends you will want to have on hand to enhance those prayers.

Adding the use of these wonderful, pure oils to your prayer time will have the effect of calming and focusing your mind, and elevating your frequency, thus helping you to feel more connected with our Creator.

"If you are having success with prayer alone, it can be increased by the intelligent use of oils. If you are having success with oils, apply them with prayer and you will see even greater success."

—David Stewart, PhD, Healing Oils of the Bible

"The effectual fervent prayer of a righteous man availeth much."

—James 5:16

PART ONE

HOW ESSENTIAL OILS ENHANCE PRAYER

Happiness on the Path

How Essential Oils Enhance Prayer

To some it might seem like a bold claim to say that essential oils can enhance prayer! They might be thinking, "How so? Convince me!" In fact, you might be thinking you would like to understand how this is possible.

Recently there has been a tremendous surge in the popularity of essential oils. While it's exciting that people are choosing a more natural way over using chemical products, unfortunately with the increase in popularity and demand there has also been a huge influx of inferior product. There are no set standards for producing oils, so it's imperative to know and trust the company you purchase your oils from, and that they are completely dedicated to purity throughout the entire process. Among people who consider themselves "oilers" (people who use essential oils), you will find everything from the occasional user or someone who just likes the way they smell, to those who are totally in love with them, study everything they can get their hands on about oils, and use them pretty much every day, in every way, including for therapeutic benefit.

Furthermore, among essential oil companies, you will find everything from those who mass produce oils that literally have no real value (in other words they are just a smell, and are often laden with toxins), to the world leader in purity, a company that goes far beyond industry standards by self-imposing rigorous testing and guidelines to ensure the highest quality possible.

Imagine a continuum: at one extreme is someone with no real knowledge of essential oils, and because they have no knowledge, they are OK with using less expensive, inferior oils. On the other end is someone who's very well versed on the subject and therefore insists on only the purest oils available.

←—Has No Knowledge ——————————Is Well Educated On Oils—→
←—Uses Inferior Oils ——————————Uses Superior Oils—→

Where do you fall on each of these lines?

More importantly, where do you need to be to have the most authentic experience?

Let's consider two people at opposite ends of the spectrum. On one end, we have someone who just likes the smell of oils and occasionally buys "lavender" for four dollars, perhaps at a craft store. On the other end, you have someone who has really researched essential oils, owns an entire library of references that they refer to often, and therefore insists on only the purest grade essential oils.

These two people are going to have very different experiences and results. The one using perfume grade, inferior oils will not receive any true benefit. They equate the lack of results with a lack of validity and dismiss the entire concept of using oils to support natural wellness. Sadly, they will miss out on the amazing lifestyle that the regular use of pure essential oils provides.

My intent is that the main focus of this book be the collection of prayers. However, because this book will be read by people who are at various points along that continuum, it is important to address how pure essential oils work. I want each reader, no matter where they are in their journey with essential oils, to understand the basics of why we believe essential oils can be an enhancement to our prayers. To that end, a very brief overview of some of the science around essential oils follows.

A Few of the Factors That Give Pure Essential Oils Their Efficacy:

1. Essential oils are designed by nature to support the health of the plant by carrying oxygen and nutrition to the cells of the plant, cleansing the cells of the plant, defending the plant against parasites and fungi, and protecting the plant from disease. Therefore, by design, they may do the same for us.

2. In truly pure oils, the oil you use will be <u>exactly as it was in nature</u>. Nothing is added, and nothing is taken away. This means that the many compounds that make up that oil are preserved and intact, and therefore may affect our cells in a positive way. Plants are made up of various constituents, and each constituent may provide different outcomes.[1]

3. Simply inhaling essential oils gets the molecules into the limbic system of the brain, the part of the brain where our emotions and memories are held. In this way, pure oils may help support us on an emotional level.

4. In many ways, these compounds or constituents support various healthy body systems, such as the respiratory system, the circulatory system, the digestive system, and many more ... all systems, really!

5. Everything is fundamentally energy at the core of its being. Pure essential oils are gifts from God, created by Him, and infused with His love and living energy. Our bodies are also created by God, made with His love and living energy and therefore may respond beautifully to the oils.

6. Saving the best for last: God intended that we use the plants for our well-being! Revelations 22:2 says "... and *the leaves of the trees were for the healing of the Nations.*" I don't know about you, but I literally got chills when I first read that! That alone is enough validation for me. I was already so excited about everything that I

---

[1] This is beyond the scope of this work; the reader is encouraged to do their own research. Please pray for guidance and discernment, so you are finding information that is true and correct.

was learning about essential oils,[‡] and then discovering that scripture, that was over-the-top proof that this is the way God intended it to be!

Raising your body's frequency while praying is virtually being closer to God on an energetic level, more connected to Source, and in touch with the Divine.

Armed with this understanding, let's now take a logical look at something long thought to be beyond logic: miracles.

Some believe that sickness is perhaps the result of blockage(s) in one's energetic body. There are several modalities of energy work that assist in helping people achieve better health simply by eliminating these blockages and getting their body's natural energy flowing again.

One definition of a miracle is an effect or extraordinary event in the physical world that surpasses all known human or natural powers and is ascribed to a supernatural cause. In other words, when a miracle occurs, the natural or material world is usually altered in some way.

One way we know that matter can be changed is to change its energetic structure. Is it not possible then, that changing the frequency of something (or someone) could also be effective at changing its (or their) physical structure?

Since healing ceremonies and prayers typically have the participant in an elevated energetic state (i.e. their frequency is higher than normal), I believe that this is one of the reasons that prayers are an important part of bringing about miracles: again we go back to the following factors: Belief, Intent, Energy, and Purity.

---

‡ My journey into the world of natural wellness began in 1989 when our family was faced with serious health challenges. We studied and made changes to our lifestyle because we had to, because of a very real need. I remember saying "I feel like everything we need has been provided by God, in nature, but that the information has been lost over time." This is why I love learning about the oils, and why I am passionate about teaching others—*so they are educated and empowered before they find themselves in crisis.*

Let's reconsider this formula—adding to it God's gift of pure essential oils:

Belief: the belief that God hears us, loves us and answers prayers, combined with the belief that essential oils can contribute to our overall well-being and a provide a closer energetic connection to God.

Intent: intentional, heartfelt, prayerful request, combined with the intentional application of pure essential oils.

Energy: the frequency of your own body, combined with that of your pure essential oils.

Purity: the purity of your own heart, combined with the purity of your essential oils.

$$\text{Belief + Intent + Energy + a Pure Heart + Pure Oils = Highly Effective Prayers}$$

I would also add Gratitude to that equation, as I believe all prayers should come from a place of gratitude—for our very lives, and for the ability to approach our Creator and talk to Him on a personal level.

We have only very briefly touched on several factors that provide scientific evidence that there is much more to using essential oils than just the scent. There are many parts to the equation that make your oils effective: God's design and direction, the properties and benefits of the constituents, the importance of purity ... and so much more[2].

For me, deep, genuine appreciation comes with this knowledge. It's extraordinary, really—nothing short of miraculous.

---

[2] Unfortunately, rules and guidelines for sharing do not allow me to reference my resources. The reader is encouraged to prayerfully do their own research.

My desire is that having this foundational understanding will make all the difference as you go into the next section. There you will find the collection of prayers, and you will have a solid base of sincere gratitude and appreciation as you recite the prayers and apply your pure essential oils.

PART TWO

PRAYERS FOR SPECIFIC NEEDS

Infinite Abundance

ABUNDANCE

"I come that they might have life, and have it more abundantly."

—John 10:10

"Not what we have, but what we enjoy, that constitutes our abundance."

—Epicurus

"The wise man does not lay up his own treasures. The more he gives to others, the more he has for his own."

—Lao Tzu

"He who is plenteously provided from within, needs but little from without."

—Johann Wolfgang Von Goethe

"Abundance is not something we acquire, it's something we tune in to."

—Wayne Dyer

"He who has God finds he lacks nothing."

—Unknown

"Joy, living in the moment, plus lack of fear equals abundance."

—Thomas Powell

ABUNDANCE

Dear God,

Thank You for Your word—guiding and teaching us as we make our journey through life.

I call upon You for Your abundant, boundless, loving provision and support: financially and in all other ways.

Lord, You are limitless. Nature demonstrates abundance and perfect provision as well as balance and harmony.

I choose to trust You and Your perfect design, not just for my life, but for all of life! I choose abundance! I choose ease. I choose joy and laughter and love in my life!

Help me to live my life as a testament to Your loving goodness, kindness and eternal support.

Thank You, I love You. I am ever so grateful.

Amen

Dear God,

Thank You for a life filled with Abundance. I am Blessed.

Thank You, I love You. I am so very grateful.

Amen

Dear God,

Thank You for Your amazing, abundant, beautiful world of nature!

Help me to remember my connection to Spirit and to the natural world: loved and supported from heaven above and the earth below!

May I see everything through the eyes of love.

May I feel everything through the energy of love.

You, and Your world are truly amazing.

Thank You, I love You. I am grateful.

Amen

Dear God,

I often feel that it's selfish or greedy to ask for (or even to desire) abundance. My life is so abundantly blessed already, that it somehow seems wrong to want more of the "good things" of life. But Father God, in Your word it says that Jesus came to earth so that we might have life, and have life more abundantly.

We know that there is more to having an abundant life than having a lot of money, but at the same time, anyone would agree that having abundance in the area of finance is certainly an important part of an abundant life.

Somehow, I have been given to believe that wanting money, receiving money, or having money are not "good" things. I now realize that wanting to be "good," and do what's right in Your eyes has created a deeply held stronghold, an internal conflict that has subconsciously limited me in this regard. Though intellectually I know that there is no basis for it, I have unconsciously believed throughout my life that I cannot be a good person and at the same time have a lot of money ... that the two are mutually exclusive.

Even now, being aware of this dichotomy, there are still conflicting messages that need to be eliminated—if I am to be free to receive my promised blessings, and use them to further serve others.

Lord, You speak easily of abundant life, prosperity, and receiving as ours—with right understanding, right mind, and right work. You speak of loving service. If there is one thing I believe, it is that I am on this earth to serve with love. I believe that much of my work provides unique, loving service to the world—one, two, (or many) people at a time!

So, loving service is definitely of great value, and value is worthy of pay. Pay in exchange for loving service is then acceptable. I accept and receive money for the value of the loving service that I render. I realize now that this is a correct, spiritually aligned principle. Thank You!

My prayer is that I can now release and re-frame those incorrect, limiting beliefs that no longer serve me (or those I would be of service to). Help me to see that accepting abundant financial blessings in exchange for right work and loving service is not only acceptable, but is the way it should be.

Having more enables me to do more and help more people. I am full of life's abundance. I am full of gratitude for this new understanding. I am excited for what the future holds!

Thank You, I love You, I am so very grateful.

Amen

Dear God,

Thank You for this beautiful time of year—today is the Spring Equinox! All around me nature is celebrating new life: birds are singing, flowers are blooming, animals scurrying around, playfully enjoying themselves in the sunshine!

Wonderful nature, exhibiting beautiful abundance—just the way You created it Lord.

Your creation, full of Your abundant life force, exploding all around me! I watch as nature operates without effort, and I see how each creature is taken care of in perfect balance and harmony.

It occurs to me now that I am also just as much a part of Your amazing design that we call nature. The same incredible, abundant life force that drives all creatures to thrive is also in me. I have the same energy and drive, the same power within me to create my own beautiful, abundant life, and I am thrilled with expectancy!

Thank You, Thank You, Thank You. I love You, I am grateful.

Amen

ACCEPTANCE

"A friend is one that knows you as you are, understands where you have been, accepts what you have become and still, gently allows you to grow."

—William Shakespeare

"Once we accept our limits, we go beyond them."

—Albert Einstein

"The only tyrant I accept in this world is the still small voice within."

—Mahatma Gandhi

"Out beyond ideas of wrongdoing and right doing, there is a field. I will meet you there."

—Rumi

"Let go of what you think life should be, so you can experience the life you have."

—Rhonda Britton

"If I could define enlightenment briefly, I would say that it is the quiet acceptance of what is."

—Wayne Dyer

Dear God,

Today I would like to talk to You about my path here while on Your beautiful earth.

At this stage of my life, I can look both forward and back in time, and I have enough experience that I can now see patterns in my life. I strive to have living for You as my "center," and have always desired to live a lifestyle that exemplifies that. Looking back now, however, it's clear to see the times that I was "off course."

I am reminded of the famous labyrinth at the Cathedral in Chartres France, the path full of winding turns that often seemed to be leading me away from the center, but that ultimately did in fact lead me back around to that very center.

I appreciate having had that experience of walking the labyrinth because I can bring that into my life now. I can see with a larger perspective, understanding that at those times when I seemed to be "off course" in the past, I was still on my path, and that it was all part of making me who I am—part of lessons learned and experiences gained. And just like in the labyrinth, I can now see that those winding, "backwards" parts of the path were still ultimately leading me to my center.

As I now look to the future, I sincerely desire to be focused, on task, purpose driven, efficient and productive! Just like in the labyrinth, the goal seems closer and more attainable, the laps seem shorter, and time itself seems to go faster as I near the center.

So, what of this stage of my life? If I could ask one thing only, I would ask for Your divine, loving, supportive guidance and help in achieving my destiny.

I want most of all to make a significant difference in the world—in people's daily lives and in their hearts and minds, to give them peace, contentment, happiness, self-worth, and love ... To leave a legacy of love, art, beauty, and writings designed with that end in mind.

I thank You for the talents You have given me, and for the burning desire to share them with the world! Let me be at peace with the twists and turns, knowing that, as with the labyrinth, it's all part of my path.

I lovingly accept my life as it is now, and I have a strong vision for how powerful it will be in the near future.

This is my prayer: for peace, acceptance, and contentment now, and Your divine help in achieving much in the days ahead.

Thank You, I love You, I am grateful.

Amen

Dear God,

Help me learn to trust (even appreciate?) the tests and difficulties along my path, knowing that I am learning, growing, and developing spiritually with each challenge that presents itself.

I trust Your perfect plan for my life. I relax and surrender into that trust, in complete acceptance, knowing that You are always in control, designing and implementing a plan that is so amazing—unfathomably superior to my plan!

Thank You, I love You. I am grateful.

Amen

ACCEPTANCE

Dear God,

I accept Your gift of a life full of abundance.

Thank You, I love You, I am grateful

Amen

Dear God,

There are parts of my life that don't seem to make sense to me. Please help me to accept them as having their place and purpose along the way.

I release the need to control so many aspects of my life that really aren't worth the time, energy, and effort required, especially when they are out of my control anyway.

I accept. I trust.

Thank You, I love You, I am grateful.

Amen

ACCEPTANCE

Dear God,

Please help me manage my time, my interests, my desires and my goals.

So many un-read books, un-written books, un-taught workshops, trips yet taken, projects yet begun ...

I'm torn between the constant need to push ahead, power through, learn more, do more, be more, and the need to slow down, rest, be at peace and be content.

Is it possible to relax into allowing accomplishments to manifest? To work less and achieve more? At this point in my life, it is not only a worthy ideal, it's a necessity.

Lord, please, I need to see results of my work. And I need to slow down, rest, and enjoy the simple things.

Oh Lord, please show me the way to accomplish more with less effort (or at least focused and productive effort), and with less stress. I accept each and every part of the path that makes up my life.

Thank You, I love You. I am grateful.

Amen

AWAKENING

"What is necessary to change a person is to change his awareness of himself."
—Abraham Maslow

"Joy in looking and comprehending is Nature's most beautiful gift."
—Albert Einstein

"The awareness of our own strength makes us modest."
—Paul Cezanne

"Awake, awake, put on your strength O Zion."
—Isaiah 52:1

"A single event can awaken within us a stranger totally unknown to us. To live is to be slowly born."
—Antoine de Saint-Exupery

"Your greatest awakening comes when you are aware about your infinite nature."
—Amit Ray

Dear God,

Thank You for giving us the things we need so that we can assist in raising the awareness of the people on this planet: wonderful teachers, books, videos, personal experiences and life lessons, dreams and visions, even clean food and water, and our wonderful oils!

Our culture has been off track for too long, and I am so excited to be witnessing an awakening and a return to natural, pure, simple, honest ways of living.

I pray that more and more people learn, grow, and share what it means to live their best lives now.

May it please You to see people return to love and service, and to let go of the silly distractions that keep us from Your best design for our lives.

Let me be an instrument for You along these lines— teaching, guiding, awakening, and helping many!

Thank You, I love You. I am blessed. I am grateful.

Amen

Dear God,

Awaken the people of the world! Awaken them to an understanding of what is true and real and important in life, recognizing that this life is such an amazing gift that we have been given!

Many are stuck: in drama, poor habits, pharmaceuticals or illegal drugs, abusive situations, Hollywood sensationalism, alcohol, nutritionally deficient food choices, co-dependency … the list goes on and on.

Toxins and stress have blocked the clear thinking necessary to find a better way. The world needs clarity!

Awaken all people to better choices: cleaner living, healthier diets, natural living, respecting and valuing our bodies, and life in general!

Empower those who desire to make these changes, and help us all to focus on the good in the world. Help us to be beacons of light, and to show love to all we come across, leaving the world a bit better with each day we live, each encounter we have.

Thank You, I love You, I am grateful.

Amen

Dear God,

Awaken in me whatever needs to be in order to accomplish my highest potential, my destiny ... Your plan for my life.

Perhaps it's confidence, knowledge, passion, determination, physical strength and energy, drive, persistence, initiative, or courage ...

Lord God, I feel like I have so many great ideas, and I truly believe in them all—that they would be beneficial to many people and help create great positive change in the world! I am definitely motivated by the desire to help others in a big way.

Sometimes I feel "stuck" at that point—in the idea stage. I ask for a touch of Your favor in actually bringing about the plans that would be valuable enough to help many people. Show me the way, provide the answers and the guidance and I will take the steps! I'm excited to know You are there to help make the way clear.

Awaken whatever needs to be awakened within me to bring these great ideas for positive change into fruition!

Thank You, I love You, I am grateful.

Amen

Dear God,

Awaken in me an awareness of Your perfect design; for my life, my work, my health, my relationships ... everything!

Awaken my spirit to be in tune with and receptive to Your perfect design. Bring me to a state of being continually aware of You in my day to day life.

I clearly see Your hand at work in my life, and it thrills me! What some may call coincidence or serendipity, I know has Your loving, intelligent, divine design behind it.

So many times, someone has casually mentioned exactly what I needed to hear, at exactly the right time and place. As a result I have been able to accomplish things that otherwise would never have happened! Recalling a few examples now, these important (and even life-saving!) messages are clear indicators of how You are active in our daily lives, watching over us with Your loving guidance.

So Lord, I know that it's possible—even highly desirable—to be awakened and connected to You and this ever available loving guidance. But sometimes our "human-ness" takes over and we forget that You are always with us, and we try to navigate our days on our own.

It's as ridiculous, really, as an amateur artist trying to improve upon one of the great masterpieces; foolishly thinking that they know enough to even try, and certainly not understanding or appreciating that the Master's work was already perfect. The audacity!

Help me to realize that my own efforts at controlling and directing my life, instead of trusting You and allowing You to guide and direct my path, would be just as arrogant and ridiculous.

Keep me awakened to the bigger picture, to Your love, and Your perfect design for my life. I ask for Your clear guidance, direction and protection as I seek to grow in loving service and pursue my purpose here. I trust You to lead me to the desired outcome.

Thank You, I am grateful. I love You.

Amen

BALANCE

"For everything there is a season, and a time for every matter under heaven: A time to be born, and a time to die; a time to plant, and a time to pluck up what it planted; a time to kill, and a time to heal; a time to break down, and a time to build up; a time to weep, and a time to laugh; a time to mourn, and a time to dance; a time to cast away stones, and a time to gather stones together; a time to embrace, and a time to refrain from embracing"

—Ecclesiastes 3: 1-8

"A false balance is an abomination to the Lord, but a just weight is His delight."

—Proverbs 11:1

"Happiness is not a matter of intensity, but of balance, order, rhythm, and harmony."

—Thomas Merton

"Mathematics expresses values that reflect the cosmos, including orderliness, balance, harmony, logic and abstract beauty."

—Deepak Chopra

"What is joy without sorrow? What is success without failure? What is a win without a loss? What is health without illness? You have to experience each if you are to appreciate the other."

—Mark Twain

BALANCE

Dear God,

I love how full my life is!

I do truly enjoy being there for the people I love: my family and friends and my business associates. And I want to be always available and supportive to them all. But sometimes it can become overwhelming. It can seem like everything and everyone else takes priority, leaving me tired and drained—physically, mentally and emotionally, even spiritually.

Please help me to find a way to accomplish all that needs to be done, and to be that loving support to those I love, while taking great care of myself with proper nutrition, rest, exercise and the luxury of options for enjoying free time.

Lord I need time for my own creativity: to paint, to write, to just enjoy the beach, and to read. And I need time to "just be" with my family, and my closest friends.

I know that in order to help others, I have to first be in a strong place myself. I ask You to help me keep this understanding in mind as I learn to manage my time and energy.

Thank You, I love You. I am so very grateful!

Amen

Dear God,

I am an empath, which allows me to feel so very much.

At times, I see this as a true gift, as I am able to relate to people in a deep and meaningful way, really understanding and feeling their point of view.

Other times, it can be overpowering, and seems to drain me on many levels.

Please encircle me with Your divine love and protection, allowing me to be of service without becoming personally exhausted.

I desire to be a lightworker for You—please help by protecting me emotionally, spiritually, energetically and physically. I trust that You are keeping me healthy and safe on all levels as I set out to love and to serve.

Thank You, I love You. I am grateful.

Amen

BALANCE

Dear God,

Thank You for Your amazing, abundant world! For the many different life forms You created in both the plant and animal kingdoms. Even in the mineral world there is such diversity and beauty. And thank You that much of it can be beneficial to our health and well-being, and that this lost information is now coming back into our awareness.

How could anyone doubt a loving, divine, intelligent creative force when contemplating the magnitude of it all? Such balance and harmony is truly awe inspiring.

What a joy to be a part of it all!

May we all live in awareness and appreciation of how miraculous our very lives are, Lord, and therefore always be conscious of living on purpose, and for You.

Thank You, I love You. I am so very grateful.

Amen

Dear God,

No doubt I am ambitious and driven, which I suppose are good traits to have, but I also need to relax and practice peace and contentment with where I am right now, in the present moment.

Help me to realize that there needs to be a healthy balance and that being quiet, peaceful and calm are a necessary and restorative part of my ideal day. That it's OK to be at rest, enjoying the waves, the breeze, the sand, the birds … and really doing nothing else!

Thank You for the opportunity to do this, and the awareness of the necessity of doing this. Your world is truly amazing and I am in awe!

Thank You, I love You. I am grateful.

Amen

BALANCE

Dear God,

Thank You for this beautiful, unexpected rain, and the powerful wind, bringing with it the most amazing smell: the clean, fresh, purifying scent of rain filled air!

I am reminded that Your perfect design for the planet and the natural world is amazing—everything in perfect balance.

So too then, Your design for my life: perfectly orchestrated and moving toward balance.

I am hopeful and excited to see what the future brings!

Thank You, I love You. I am grateful.

Amen

BELIEVE

"Once we believe in ourselves, we can risk curiosity, wonder, spontaneous delight, or any experience that reveals the human spirit."

—E.E. Cummings

"You are a valuable, worthwhile human being—not because anybody says so, not because you're successful, not because you made a lot of money—but because you decide to believe it and for no other reason."

—Wayne Dyer

"Your chances of success in any undertaking can always be measured by your belief in yourself."

—Robert Collier

"I am a success today because I had a friend who believed in me and I didn't have the heart to let him down."

—Abraham Lincoln

"All personal breakthroughs begin with a change in belief."

—Anthony Robbins

Dear God,

I believe that the dreams and goals in my heart were given by You. I believe that I am well equipped to accomplish these aspirations. Further, I believe that it is my responsibility to achieve them.

In faith, I claim all right ideas, inspirations, empowerment, energy, fortitude, and fortuitous encounters ... in other words, I claim Your anointing over and blessing on my every endeavor.

I see the dream becoming a reality. I see many people being helped and I see these efforts making a significant, positive difference in the world!

I believe my life and my work are highly favored and blessed for inevitable success.

Thank You, I love You. I am ever grateful.

Amen

Dear God,

My deepest desire is to be living "on purpose" and to achieve my destiny. I too often get sidetracked (by fear, honestly) when I start to feel like I need to "get a real job, and earn a regular paycheck." I suppose it's just part of being human, as we need income to live.

It MUST be possible to earn a living while pursuing what I truly believe in, or that desire would not be so strong in my heart. I feel like it's a test of sorts, to see how committed I am to my truth. Please make the way clear!

I am truly inspired and so very motivated. I am doing the actual work. Please Lord, bless these efforts!

Thank You, I love You. I am grateful.

Amen

Dear God,

Thank You for clear evidence that You are in control! I trust that I can go forward with confidence, and remain happy and at peace, regardless of appearances.

I trust completely. I take refuge in the assurance that You know far better than I do what is best in any situation.

Thank You, I love You. I am grateful.

Amen

Dear God,

I have so many ideas! There are so many things I want to do, create and accomplish!

Please guide me, help me to know where to begin, help me to stay focused and bring them to fruition. Help me to use my time wisely. Connect me to the right people at the right time, and give me the means to make the dreams become reality!

I long to hear "Well done, good and faithful servant!"

With Your help and guidance, I am so excited to see what unfolds as we go along together into the (near!) future.

Thank You, I love You. I am grateful beyond measure.

Amen

BUILDING YOUR DREAM

"I wake every morning feeling like I am living in a miracle, where spirituality, creativity, work and love have all come to mean the same thing."

—Deva Premal

"I can do all things through Christ who strengthens me."

—Phillipians 4:13

"All things are possible to him that believeth."

—Mark 9:23

"And we know that all things work together for good to them that love God, and are called according to His purpose."

—Romans 8:28

"Now unto Him that is able to do exceedingly, abundantly, above and beyond all that we ask or think, according to the power that worketh in us."

—Ephesians 3:20,21

"Consult not your fears but your hopes and dreams. Concern yourself not with what you have tried and failed in, but with what is still possible for you to do."

—Pope John XXIII

"Cherish your visions and your dreams as they are the children of your soul, the blueprints of your ultimate achievements."

—Napoleon Hill

"You control your future, your destiny. What you think about comes about. By recording your dreams and goals on paper, you set in motion the process of becoming the person you most want to be. Put your future in good hands—your own.

—Mark Victor Hansen

BUILDING YOUR DREAM

Dear God,

I call upon You; Your infinite love and knowledge to guide my every step as I set out to achieve the dreams that You have placed in my heart.

I pray for clear focus and inspiration for exactly the correct thing, whether a collection of writings, new pieces of art, or sharing Your amazing oils as a natural way to support wellness ...

These are the things I love, the things I am passionate about, Lord. I truly believe in them, and I believe that the world needs them and will be better for having them! Please give me the inspiration in each and every moment, to know which to be working on and how I can help others.

In addition to inspiration, I ask for the motivation and focus to make it happen. With Godly inspiration, motivation, and passion, I believe that success is inevitable!

I am grateful for the talent, the passion and the drive that You have given me. You are indeed an awesome, loving Father who has provided me with everything I need. It is now up to me to put the dream into action! I pray that You bless my efforts and my work. Bless the people whose lives I touch through my art, my writing, and my teaching.

What a beautiful, inspired, joy filled way to live life!
Where spirituality, creativity, work and love are all one
and the same. That defines Heaven on earth!

Thank You, I love You. I am so very grateful!

Amen

Dear God,

There are not words to adequately express how grateful I am for my life—the entirety of it, and all the blessings that You have given me.

It is from this place of sincere gratitude that I desire to give back to You—to live for You, Lord. My heart is pure in that desire, and my mind is clear … I ask only that You make known to me what that highest calling would be, and show me how to attain that goal.

Enlighten me. Empower me. I am willing and ready to put the necessary work into bringing it about.

Motivate me. Inspire me. May there be no shortage of unique and wonderful ideas of ways to help people all around the world to improve their lives!

I see many people's lives improving, as they learn to make better choices and find ways to achieve wellness, guided by their love for You and appreciation for Your provision through nature.

Please show me the path, the plan and the people needed and help me generate the resources to bring it to life!

Help me to show people how to overcome the current paradigm of being out of balance and depleted, and show them instead how to bring joy, balance, well-being, and happiness back into their lives.

Help me to help people connect to You, God, to source, to love, to return to the original AWE-some-ness that we were born with, and created to be!

Thank You, I love You. I am grateful.

Amen

Dear God,

Thank You for Your loving divine guidance in my life.

Thank You for Your patience as I learn to trust that guidance. Thank You for signs along the way that clearly point me in the best direction. Help me to become more aware of these gentle nudges and chance meetings, looking for You in them, showing me which path to choose.

It's so exciting to be tuned in and actually watch Your hand at work.

I trust You God.

Thank You, I love You. I am grateful.

Amen

Dear God,

Please help me to manage my time in a better way. I do understand the value of my time; once spent, it cannot be replenished or earned back.

You know me, Lord—typically too easily distracted, too little focus and too many things pulling at me.

I sincerely ask that You help me become more focused and results oriented. Help me take my ideas to completion so that many can learn, enjoy and benefit from what I can offer.

Help me to know with clarity which things to say "yes" to and which ones should be a gracious or gentle "no, thank you," thus protecting my time for the most important things.

Please assist me in achieving a level of financial security where money is abundant, enough, and flowing easily so that the pressure to earn more will be removed, freeing me to spend my time doing the things that I love, and that I feel like will benefit many people.

Thank You, I love You. I am grateful.

Amen

Dear God,

Today I come to You with even more gratitude, and even more appreciation for my healthy body, indeed my life. The gift of the here and now is amazing beyond words.

When faced with a potential threat, an unknown that could derail all my plans, and faced with the possibility of having to fight for my own survival, everything previously taken for granted becomes precious! My family visiting and to hear them laughing—a wonderful gift! The taste of good, clean food, well prepared—a joy!

While we believe ourselves to be grateful and appreciative at all times, the threat that it all could be taken away is a great catalyst for taking that gratitude to new heights! Oh, how everything precious is then truly seen as such, and everything unimportant also falls to its proper place.

Today, I am so very grateful to You for that. I also want to make sure that I express deep and sincere gratitude for everyone You have placed in my life. Thank You for everything that has brought me to this time and place.

Assist me in going forward boldly! No more wasted time! Time for action. Time for results. Time to make every day count.

Thank You, I love You. I am so very grateful. I am blessed beyond measure.

Amen

Dear God,

Today I pray for anyone who is struggling with health issues: physical, mental, or emotional.

Be with them and comfort them wherever they are in the process, and surround them with Your love.

Please Lord, look at their situations, and if You see it as best for them, please send them healing.

Unfortunately, many of us take for granted our health, until it becomes an issue, so perhaps gaining a perspective of appreciation is part of the lesson. Having learned appreciation for a healthy body, please let them be healed, and free to enjoy life and live for You, God.

Thank You for a healthy body, and for the physical strength and energy to live my life to it's fullest.

And thank You for each new day in this healthy body—the gift of time to accomplish my goals and to bring about the dreams that You have placed in my heart.

Thank You, I love You. I am so very grateful.

Amen

Dear God,

I want to understand clearly when You are speaking to me. I am paying attention (or at least, I'm trying to!), my eyes and ears are open, searching …

Please show me the best way forward—every minute of every day.

I have grown to become very aware of the value of my time, and want to use it for Your loving service, Lord.

With Your clear guidance and direction, and Your helping hand, I am excited to see what can be accomplished!

Thank You, I love You. I am grateful.

Amen

CLARITY

"Everyone sees the unseen in proportion to the clarity of his heart."

—Rumi

"I experience a period of frightening clarity in those moments when nature is so beautiful."

—Vincent Van Gogh

"Truth is by nature self-evident. As soon as you remove the cobwebs of ignorance that surround it, it shines clear."

—Mahatma Gandhi

"Clarity of mind means clarity of passion ..."

—Blaise Pascal

"Clarity affords focus."

—Thomas Leonard

Dear God,

As I am becoming more and more aware of subtle energies and how I am (greatly) affected by them, I ask for Your guidance and protection over me—body, mind, spirit, and energy field.

Help me see clearly what is beneficial to me, and what is not, and help me to implement any necessary changes in order to have the most sublime life now, and into the future!

Also, may I be a guide, showing others how to do the same, through my art, my writing, and Your amazing essential oils.

Help me create and maintain an environment—at home and at work—that is conducive to peace, relaxation, joy, creativity, inspiration, love, happiness, and bliss here on earth. Love, Love, Love.

Thank You, I love You. I am grateful.

Amen

Dear God,

Please increase my awareness of what is good and right and true in this life. Of what is actually important, as opposed to just urgent.

Let me be a beacon of light to those in darkness, and a helper and a friend to those who need hope, a smile, or maybe just an encouraging word.

Give me eyes to see and ears to hear the truth, and the energy, resources and time to help those in need.

Thank You, I love You. I am blessed. I am grateful.

Amen

Dear God,

It seems that as I get older, my focus changes, and what seemed urgent in the past no longer does. What I now know is of utmost importance is to love and serve You, God, first, and my family, and all Your creation. Thank You for increasing my clarity and helping me grow in wisdom.

Please now, help me share my love and my gifts with the world in a big way, so that many people's lives are improved.

Thank You, I love You. I am grateful.

Amen

Dear God,

Thank You for a perfectly functioning, healthy body! Thank You that every system is designed to operate with perfection and in constant communication with every other system; the reality of this body is miraculous beyond comprehension!

Today, I pray that You give me the focus, determination and strength to bring my physical body to its highest potential, in every aspect, through exercise, proper nutrition, and adequate rest.

May the recognition of the miracle that my body is give me clarity as to why I need to honor and care for it with diligence.

May awareness of Your Spirit in me give me the desire to treat my body with love and respect, keeping it in optimal condition and worthy of Your dwelling.

Thank You for the miracle of this body for my time on earth. Thank You for my continued good health!

Thank You, I love You, I am ever so grateful.

Amen

ENVISION

"The great thing in the world is not so much where we stand, as in what direction we are moving."

—Oliver Wendell Holmes

"Vision without action is a daydream. Action without vision is a nightmare."

—Japanese Proverb

"Create a vision, and never let the environment, other people's beliefs, or the limits of what has been done in the past shape your decisions."

—Anthony Robbins

"To come to be, you must have a vision of Being, a Dream, a Purpose, and Principle. You will become what your vision is."

—Peter Zarlenga

"A man, to carry on a successful business, must have imagination. He must see things as in a vision, a dream of the whole thing."

—Charles Schwab

"The vision must be followed with venture. It's not enough to stare up the steps, we must step up the stairs."

—Vance Havner

Dear God,

May we all, collectively, envision a beautiful and peaceful world where all people are loving and compassionate, treating everyone with genuine concern and respect,

A world where animal life is valued and revered, and all animals are also treated with love and compassion,

A world where people do the right thing, simply because it is the right thing to do,

A world where the highest and best purpose that anyone can aspire to is to be of loving service to all life forms as a form of respect for their creator,

And a world where the most urgent thing anyone can want is to seek to grow closer to that loving creator: You, God.

Please, as more and more enlightened people share this vision, may this expedite it becoming our new reality!

Thank You, I love You. I am grateful.

Amen

Dear God,

Help all who understand their powerful potential to create positive change to collectively and continuously envision a world where love is the only force in action,

Where everyone considers the thoughts, feelings and needs of others,

Where people work together toward a common higher good,

Where there is no need for fighting or war,

Where it is everyone's true pleasure to help their family, friends and neighbors, simply for the joy they receive by helping and giving to others!

As we seek You, and that daily relationship with You becomes stronger, help us to be cognizant of how our thoughts and actions contribute to the betterment of the planet.

Let us all envision peace, love, health, freedom, joy and happiness for all!

Thank You, I love You. I am so very grateful.

Amen

Dear God,

Today I ask that You honor the work that I do, and that many people are blessed by it.

You have taught us that it is Your desire that we live a full and abundant life. Help us to understand and fully realize what this means, and come into complete alignment with it, so that we can experience that which is our own best life!

Thank You for the people that I come into contact with, that You send my way Lord, and thank You for allowing me to be that vehicle by which they learn, grow and become empowered to live their own best lives: spiritually, mentally, emotionally, physically, and even financially!

We desire first and foremost Your design for our lives, and want to be of loving service each and every day.

Thank You, I love You. I am so very grateful!

Amen

FORGIVENESS

"In him we have redemption through his blood, the forgiveness of sins, in accordance with the riches of God's grace."

—Ephesians 1:7

"To err is human, to forgive, Divine."

—Alexander Pope

"The practice of forgiveness is our most important contribution to the healing of the world."

—Marianne Williamson

"The best thing you can give to your enemy is forgiveness; to an opponent, tolerance; to a friend, your heart; to your child, a good example; to a father, deference; to your mother, conduct that will make her proud of you; to yourself, respect; to all men, charity."

—Benjamin Franklin

"Newton, forgive me."

—Albert Einstein

"To understand everything is to forgive everything."

—Buddha

Dear God,

I come to You humbly, seeking Your loving forgiveness. There have been times that I've fallen short, and situations where I've chosen the wrong course of action, or caused someone pain (even if unintentional). There have been times that I wasn't the witness or example that I should have been for You.

I know it's all part of our human-ness and that everyone makes mistakes at times, but I ask that You please find it in Your omnipotence and grace to grant me the peace that comes from knowing that You have forgiven me.

By the same token, I forgive anyone who has caused me pain, or wronged me in any perceived way. I release "the story" and any negative emotions attached to it, as well as the need to be "made right."

I give forgiveness. I accept forgiveness.

Thank You, I love You, I am so very grateful.

Amen

Dear God,

Thank You for Your liberating gift of forgiveness, removing our downfalls "as far as the East is from the West."

Your forgiveness is the largest part of emotional freedom from shame and guilt, but I also need to forgive myself. Please help me to see myself through Your patient, kind, loving eyes: as having worth and value, as forgiven and clean, whole and healthy!

Thank You, I love You, I am grateful.

Amen

Dear God,

Can it be that giving forgiveness is even more liberating that being forgiven? It seems to be the case.

Thank You for Your forgiveness.

I forgive others, and I forgive myself.

Thank You, I love You. I am grateful.

Amen

Dear God,

Please forgive the wasted time, the lack of understanding and lack of focus in my life up to now.

Please assist me in staying on course going forward in a powerful way!

Thank You, I love You. I am grateful.

Amen

FORGIVENESS

Dear God,

Today, may I see everyone as You do, as if they have already achieved their highest potential.

Help us all to forgive any current or past events or conditions that might be keeping us from being our very best to one another. Thank You for Your forgiveness! Let us not be forgetful of the amazing grace that You have shown us.

Thank You, I love You. I am grateful.

Amen

GRATITUDE

"Many times a day I realize how much of my own life is built on the labors of my fellowmen, and how earnestly I must exert myself in order to give in return as much as I have received."

—Albert Einstein

"Let us be grateful to the people who make us happy; they are the charming gardeners who make our souls bloom."

—Marcel Proust

"Do not spoil what you have by desiring what you have not; remember that what you now have was once among the things you only hoped for."

—Epicurus

"Walk as if you are kissing the earth with your feet."

—Thich Nhat Hahn

"Piglet noticed that though he had a very small heart, it could hold a rather large amount of gratitude."

—A.A. Milne

"Cultivate the habit of being grateful for every good thing that comes to you, and give thanks continuously. And because all things have contributed toward your advancement, you should include all things in your gratitude."

—Ralph Waldo Emerson

Dear God,

Thank You for a beautiful life! Thank You for an amazing, loving family. Thank You for a beautiful home and plenty of food. Thank You for a partner who loves and appreciates me, and fully supports my endeavors. Thank You for our amazing, wonderful children and the pleasure of seeing them grow into adults that we are so proud of. Thank You for our sweet, loving pet, and the joy she brings to our home.

Thank You for Your love, Your care, and always for Your infinite, abundant supply for all our needs. Thank You for Your patience, Your forgiveness, and Your gentle, loving guidance.

Thank You for my path, my life lessons, and for bringing me through to the peaceful place I am today.

Thank You for all of the truly special people in my life: family, friends, acquaintances, co-workers, and the rare "instant connection" with some that can only be described as divinely orchestrated.

Thank You for my unique talents and abilities, and the strong desire to help others that has allowed me to grow into sharing and teaching.

Thank You for the unending inspiration, and the drive to start, persevere, and see through to completion all of my "big ideas" for making the world a better place:

one offering at a time, one gift at a time, one person at a time, one class at a time, one day at a time.

Thank You for the belief in my dreams and my purpose that pushes me to continue on. Thank You for the motivation and encouragement, and for putting me in front of exactly the right person at the right time so that amazing things transpire—evidence of Your love and support.

Thank You for my newfound clear understanding of the universal principles of energy and attraction. Thank You for faith in myself, my gifts and my talents, and in the people of the world to receive them with excitement, enthusiasm and appreciation.

Thank You, Thank You, Thank You! I am grateful. I love You.

Amen

Dear God,

Thank You for providing all that we need for a healthy, happy, and prosperous life!

Your beautiful world is amazing, God! Full of gifts for those who can see.

Thank You, I love You. I am blessed. I am grateful.

Amen

Dear God,

Thank You for the sum total of my life's experiences that have made me who I am today!

Looking back, I have no doubt that every part has been Divinely guided—all for good, easing me ever onward toward Your highest plan for my life.

I thank You for Your forgiveness, for Your continued guidance and support, and for Your constant love.

Thank You, I love You. I am humbled and grateful.

Amen

GRATITUDE

Dear God,

Thank You for my perfectly healthy body,

For eyes that see with focus and vision,

For ears that hear with clarity, the truth,

For a heart that beats strong and steady, full of Love,

For all systems working optimally, and in harmony,

For strong legs and sure feet that carry me along Your path,

For arms and hands that effortlessly facilitate Your loving work.

Thank You, God, for the continued health and strength that I enjoy in the miracle that I call my body.

May I use it long and well, and with great care and appreciation, as I strive to be a vehicle of Your love on this plane, offering help and loving service to others.

Thank You, I love You. I am blessed. I am grateful.

Amen

Dear God,

Please: clean air, pure food and water, clean earth, and simply loving life.

Thank You for: clean air, pure food and water, clean earth, and simply loving life!

I see beauty all around. I am filled with deep appreciation and gratitude.

Thank You, I love You. I am blessed. I am grateful.

Amen

Dear God,

I see beauty everywhere! In Nature. In Your beautiful people. In art. In laughter and joy!

Help me to keep my focus there, on the beauty, and be a shining light to help others find their own best path.

Thank You for the people in my life, the resources, the coincidences and serendipities that help me to know that You are in control and that we are doing something truly amazing together!

Thank You, I love You. I am blessed. I am grateful.

Amen

Dear God,

Who can explain the complete joy one feels upon learning that their health is still intact, life is still before them, and they can once again focus on what brings them joy and fulfillment?!

I have nothing less than deep, sincere gratitude for the miracle of life ...

I'm thrilled to be healthy, vibrant, and full of ideas for the future!

Joy overflows. Happiness all around! Sincere appreciation and love for my life!

Thank You, I love You. I am deeply grateful.

Amen

Dear God,

Thank You for a healthy body!

Thank You for Your provision of so many beautiful, clean, nutritious fruits and vegetables! And for clean, clear water, on demand anytime I want it, and at whatever temperature I need!

Thank You that I am blessed to be in an environment where food and water are plentiful, and that I have the means to choose and prepare these beautiful foods.

Today, I want to ask that all the world will awaken to better ways of being human; to put forth the most worthy goal of ending hunger and suffering.

May all the people of the world have enough good, healthy, clean food to eat, and enough clean water to drink.

Today, and every day, I am deeply aware of how very blessed I am. I pray for the means to make a significant difference in the lives of many, Lord, all around the world!

Thank You, I love You. I am grateful.

Amen

Dear God,

I thank You for a truly amazing team of people that share my vision and the goal of helping many find a better, more natural lifestyle with Your pure essential oils.

I know that You have sent each one into my life, for me to bless, and to be blessed by them. Thank You for their respect and their trust as they share their stories and their needs with me. I love every one of them—they each mean so very much to me.

I pray that You bless our entire team, Lord, each and every one, with blessings so amazing that there can be no doubt that it was because of You; so AWE-some that everyone will know that they could not have done it without Divine help.

I pray that each one sees their lives altered in a profound and positive way, so that they are free to help others even more.

I pray Your blessings and Your hand of favor over each person on my team, on all of us, Lord.

For freedom from the very real bondage of debt.

For freedom from the job that has become a tiresome grind.

For freedom from the job that lacks meaning or purpose.

For freedom from feeling stuck, and seeing no way out.

Lord, every single person that I know on my team has a wonderful, loving heart, and they want first and foremost to help others. They are so loving and nurturing, and many of them have a hard time believing that it's OK for them to be on the receiving end of love and blessings!

Please Lord, these are wonderful, giving people, and they all truly deserve to be blessed.

We have all worked hard.

We have all continued to give of ourselves, even when it's difficult to do so.

We have all given our money to help others, even when it was not easy.

We have all held on to hope.

We have all been nurturers, pouring into others, even ahead of ourselves.

We have all remained faithful.

We have all struggled long enough, Lord.

It's time to bless these dear souls. I want to pray for each one by name, and I pray that You see each and every one, see their situations. And I pray that You see that these are people that, if given time freedom and financial freedom, will use it well to continue to bless others further. They are the people that, if given the option and the means, will make a significant, positive difference in the world.

I know that with Your love, Your blessings, and Your favor, this team of amazing people will be able to do great things and help many! I love and appreciate them, every one.

I pray that You see it so.

Thank You, I love You. I am eternally grateful.

Amen

Dear God,

Instead of dreading vacuuming and dusting, let me say Thank You for a beautiful home.

Instead of being tired of doing dishes, let me say Thank You for always having good food to eat.

Instead of resisting cleaning the bathrooms, let me say Thank You for clean, hot water anytime I want it.

Instead of begrudging washing the car, let me say Thank You for a nice vehicle.

Instead of getting frustrated that I can't seem to help my dog overcome her allergies, let me say Thank You that she is still with us, and Thank You for the love and joy she brings us.

Instead of being frustrated that I don't seem to have enough free time to spend with friends and family, let me say Thank You for work, and enough money to meet our needs.

I am beginning to see that it's all just a matter of perspective, isn't it Lord? Thank You for loving me and always being patient with me as I learn and grow, if ever so slowly.

Thank You, I love You. I am so very grateful for my life, all of it.

Amen

Dear God,

Thank You for every single aspect of my life! I am grateful for all of it, the good times and the difficult times, for all of it together, all of my life experiences that have brought me to the place I am. I am who I am as a result of the entirety of it all.

I am grateful for the wonderful people in my life. I am grateful for all that I have learned. I am grateful for my abilities, and my passion and my drive.

I know that I am loved, provided for, guided and protected. I feel safe and secure. I know that whatever I set out to do can and will be accomplished! I know that I am successful.

My highest potential is already in me. I am already that—my highest potential. I feel at peace with my path. My gifts and my talents have great value, and come with a responsibility to share with others. It is time.

I feel deep gratitude. I feel excitement as I look into the future.

I feel deep joy, love and appreciation.

Thank You, I love You, I am grateful.

Amen

Dear God,

Thank You for providing all that we need for a healthy, happy, and prosperous life!

Your beautiful world is amazing God!

This life is so full of gifts for those who can see.

Thank You, I love You. I am blessed. I am grateful.

Amen

Dear God,

Today I want to say Thank You for our pet, and for the joy and love she brings into our home.

Help us to be good people for her and to show her only love and affection. She is pure hearted and innocent, and deserves nothing but gentleness and admiration, love and peace in her life.

Help us to learn from her: loyalty, patience, love, long-suffering, gratitude, gentleness, playfulness, forgiveness … and so much more.

Thank you for letting her find us, and us find her, for indeed, who has rescued who? She is a delight, pure and simple.

As she ages, I ask that she not have to deal with physical pain. She doesn't understand and we want her to be comfortable, happy, and at peace.

May we be good stewards of her life and time with us. Thank You for the blessing of being loved by, and of loving one of Your purest creations!

Thank You, I love You, I am grateful.

Amen

GROUNDING

"These are the themes in life which are consistent in Judaism, Islam, Hinduism— of being grounded in who you are and being engaged in an unjust world."

—Cory Booker

"This is a marathon in life. You can't be sprinting all the time or else you wear yourself out. You have to make sure you're taking care of yourself, keeping yourself grounded and not letting every little thing get you worked up."

—Brian Moynihan

"Honesty is grounded in humility and indeed in humiliation, and in admitting exactly where we are powerless."

—David Whyte

"The strong bond of friendship is not always a balanced equation; friendship is not always about giving and taking in equal shares. Instead, friendship is grounded in a feeling that you know exactly who will be there for you when you need something, no matter what or when."

—Simon Sinek

"Nothing profits more than self-esteem, grounded on what is just and right."

—John Milton

"Walk as if you are kissing the earth with your feet."

—Thich Nhat Hahn

Dear God,

Today is an exceptionally nice day! It started out cool in the morning, and by afternoon it's hinting at Summer! The sun is warm on my skin but not too hot, and the sky is a deep blue with not a cloud in sight!

Sometimes we forget to appreciate all of nature: beautiful days like today, and also the days with wind, rain, snowfall, thunder and lightning, all in perfect harmony.

Thank You for Your beautiful natural world! Thank You for the terrain, the oceans, the rivers and lakes, plants, animals, minerals, and the people … from the grandest to the smallest, help us to truly appreciate all of nature's gifts. And Lord, help us to always be good stewards of the earth for You.

Thank You, I love You. I am so very grateful.

Amen

Dear God,

I am in awe of Your vast creation. The grandeur of it all makes one feel small and insignificant. You are amazing, God!

Lord, I want to know Your mind, Your heart, Your thoughts. I want that day-to-day, minute-to-minute relationship with You. I want You with me always, guiding my path, giving me exactly the right the words that will help uplift or encourage someone at just the right time.

I want to feel that connection with You continually; to know that I am my higher spiritual self, my soul, my spirit, my divine consciousness, and not my physical body, my work or my possessions.

I long to make a significant difference in the lives of many.

Please keep me connected and protected as I go about searching for Your correct path for my life.

Thank You, I love You. I am ever grateful.

Amen

Dear God,

Oh! The beauty of Your creation! I am surrounded by so many plants and animals, reminding me how very vibrant life is ...

How often we forget how majestic and perfect the natural world is! We get busy going about our days, lost in "urgent" matters that most likely are not truly important.

Today I am blessed to be able to stop for a while, and just "be," in acres of beautiful gardens, with no agenda for the next few hours. I can take time, and really appreciate the beauty and the scents all around me.

How does life become so busy that we don't have time for this regularly? I'm reminded of the source of our amazing oils, and I am deeply grateful and appreciative.

Thank You for this reminder today, of how amazing You are, and how wonderful Your natural world is, how much beauty we have been given to enjoy, if we will only take notice!

Thank You, I love You. I am deeply grateful for all Your creation.

Amen

Dear God,

You are Love, and offer loving support to Your beautiful creation!

Please send a beam of Your loving energy down onto me—completely filling me, my body, every cell in my body and the spaces between the cells of my body with the energy of pure LOVE.

At the same time, let me connect to and feel the Earth's wonderful and powerful energy, coming up through me as it reaches towards You!

Let my body (and my life!) be empowered and charged by the joining of those two powerful energies: the physical and the spiritual, matter and ephemeral, Mother and Father, Nature and Heaven.

Thus empowered and divinely guided, how can I go off course as I set out to accomplish the things I shall attempt today?! Success is inevitable when correctly connected to the source of Love and power, and putting forth loving effort toward a good and correct end!

Thank You, I love You. I am grateful.

Amen

HARMONY

"Happiness is when what you think, what you say, and what you do are in harmony."

—Mahatma Gandhi

"To put everything in balance is good, to put everything in harmony is better."

—Victor Hugo

"Every now and then go away, have a little relaxation, for when you come back to your work your judgment will be surer. Go some distance away because then the work appears smaller and more of it can be taken at a glance and a lack of harmony and proportion is more readily seen."

—Leonardo da Vinci

"The outer conditions of a person's life will always be found to be harmoniously related to his inner state ... Men do not attract that which they want, but that which they are."

—James Allen

"Out of clutter find simplicity. From discord find harmony."

—Albert Einstein

"How is it they live in such harmony, the billions of stars."

—Saint Thomas Aquinas

Dear God,

I believe that You have provided all that we need in many ways, and that one of those ways is through nature. I am full of gratitude for this and am so excited to see that this "lost" knowledge is now being re-discovered and affirmed by science!

Our bodies are nothing short of miraculous! Your abundant world is the same! How could anyone doubt the existence of a loving Creator—that Divine Intelligent Designer that made everything to function in perfect harmony?

Help us to find peace in the knowledge that Your perfect design is for health, harmony, happiness and perfect balance. Help us to live in alignment with that awesome vision.

Thank You, I love You, I am grateful.

Amen

Dear God,

Thank You for this beautiful, unexpected rain, and the powerful wind, bringing with it the most amazing smell: the clean, fresh, purifying scent of rain filled air!

I am reminded that Your perfect design for the planet and the natural world is amazing—everything in perfect balance.

So too then, Your design for my life: perfectly orchestrated and moving toward balance.

I am hopeful and excited to see what the future brings!

Thank You, I love You. I am grateful.

Amen

Dear God,

Thank You for Your amazing, wonderful world! Thank You for all of nature and the perfect harmony in Your loving, divine design. Thank You for the plants, and for all that they provide for us: food, clothing, shelter and more. And thank You for the gift of the essential oils of the plants: the life essence, the living intelligence and energy that they allow us to participate in!

Your world is nothing less than awesome God, and the more I learn, the more fascinated and in awe I am!

Lord, I want everyone to know and understand how amazing Your oils are. Please open their eyes and ears and hearts to the truth, so that they experience the wonders of nature's way.

Please use me as a messenger, helping those who need Your oils, and teaching people that they have a better, more natural way to be healthy.

Guide and direct my path, oh Lord. Put me where I need to be, and in contact with those who need (and want) this information!

I'm thrilled every time someone shares a success or transformation story—no matter how small—as they learn to experiment with and trust the gift of oils that You have given to us.

I'm honored to play a part in spreading this empowering and life changing information with Your world—one day at a time, one person at a time!

Thank You for each and every step of my life's path that has brought me to where I am at the present moment.

Thank You for hope and excitement for the future, and for finding "work" that has real meaning and purpose!

Thank You, I love You. I am blessed. I am grateful.

Amen

HIGHEST PURPOSE

"You were born with potential. You were born with goodness and trust. You were born with ideals and dreams. You were born with greatness. You were born with wings. You were not meant for crawling, so don't. You have wings. Learn to use them and fly."

—Rumi

"Always dream and shoot higher than you know you can do. Do not bother just to be better than your contemporaries or predecessors. Try to be better than yourself."

—William Faulkner

"Continuous effort—not strength or intelligence—is the key to unlocking our potential."

—Winston Churchill

"Everyone has inside of him a piece of good news. The good news is that you don't know how great you can be! How much you can love! What you can accomplish! And what your potential is!"

—Anne Frank

"Success is ... knowing your purpose in life, growing to reach your maximum potential, and sowing seeds that benefit others."

—John C Maxwell

HIGHEST PURPOSE

Dear God,

I pray that above all I may reach my highest potential; that I am mindful always of You and Your perfect plan for my life.

In my parenting, my teaching, my work, my artwork, my writing, my relationships, and caring for the people in my life ... in all aspects I want love for You to shine through.

Loving Father, if I had to choose only one thing to ask, it would be this, for I believe that living a life with my highest potential as the constant goal would necessarily align everything else!

I long to hear You say, "Well done, good and faithful servant."

Thank You, I love You, I am grateful.

Amen

Dear God,

Help me to be an instrument of Your love, to be an encourager, to see people in their wholeness and perfection, as You see them, and to speak favor over everyone I meet.

May I look upon everyone with love and kindness, with a genuine smile and always ready with a hug for anyone who needs one.

Help me to help others see and choose their own path to their highest potential, health, joy, and fulfillment!

Place me where You want me, open the eyes, ears and hearts of those in need, and use my words and loving kindness to show them a better way.

Thank You, I love You. I am grateful.

Amen

Dear God,

Just one thing today: I completely accept Your plan for my life.

Thank You, I love You. I am grateful.

Amen

Dear God,

I pray for discernment.

There is so much "noise" out there, and so many distractions ...

Please guide, direct and protect me, and all those in my life, so that we can all live to our highest and best for You!

Thank You, I love You. I am grateful.

Amen

Dear God,

May I be clearly guided—day by day, moment by moment—to that goal which is my highest and best, for You, God.

Thank You, I love You. I am grateful.

Amen

Dear God,

Please give me the courage and the confidence to take the steps necessary for achieving my divine life purpose.

I pray for continued clarity as to what my highest calling is, and then guidance as to the steps toward making it a reality.

I trust that with that clear vision and steady, determined, consistent action, the goal will be attained, in Your perfect timing, Lord.

I thank You for Your loving guidance, direction and protection every day, and every step of the way.

I am excited to see what the future holds! I am deeply grateful for all that I have been blessed with. Please help me to help others awaken to their best lives as well!

Thank You, I love You. I am grateful.

Amen

Dear God,

I am in awe of Your vast creation. The grandeur of it all makes one feel small and insignificant. You are amazing, God!

Lord, I want to know Your mind, Your heart, Your thoughts. I want that day-to-day, minute-to-minute relationship with You. I want You with me always, guiding my path, giving me exactly the right the words that will help uplift or encourage someone at just the right time.

I want to feel that connection with You continually; to know that I am my higher spiritual self, my soul, my spirit, my divine consciousness, and not my physical body, my work or my possessions.

I long to make a significant difference in the lives of many.

Please keep me connected and protected as I work, and search for Your correct path for my life.

Thank You, I love You. I am ever grateful.

Amen

Dear God,

With new eyes, new understanding, and new appreciation for my life, help me to use each moment in a fully effective way; knowing who I really am, and what I am here to do, tuned in to You and Your angels for constant guidance and protection.

Thank You, I love You. I am grateful.

Amen

HOPE

"Be joyful in hope, patient in affliction, faithful in prayer."

—Romans 12:12

"Love does not delight in evil but rejoices with the truth. It always protects, always trusts, always hopes, always perseveres."

—I Corinthians 13:6,7

"It's really a wonder that I haven't dropped all my ideals, because they seem so absurd and impossible to carry out. Yet I keep them, because in spite of everything, I still believe that people are really good at heart."

—Anne Frank

"Learn from yesterday, live for today, hope for tomorrow."

—Albert Einstein

"They say a person needs just three things to be truly happy in this world: someone to love, something to do, and something to hope for."

—Tom Bodett

"... We also glory in our sufferings, because we know that suffering produces perseverance; perseverance, character; and character, hope. And hope does not put us to shame, because God's love has been poured out into our hearts through the Holy Spirit, who has been given to us."

—Romans 5:3–5

Dear God,

Thank You for a beautiful life filled with hope for the future!

I am blessed indeed, for how many can truly say that? I love my life! I am happy now, and excited and hopeful for an even better future! Awesome!

Thank You, I love You. I am grateful.

Amen

Dear God,

May I show people a way to peace, joy, love, happiness and hope!

If it's possible to paint these—I will. Please show me how!

Guide my hand, clear my vision, and inspire me Divinely.

I want my work to be inspiring, encouraging, and life changing!

Thank You, I love You. I am ever so grateful.

Amen

Dear God,

Help me to be at peace with the past, knowing that there is forgiveness, and content with the present, realizing abundant blessings, and hopeful for the future, trusting that You have my best path available to me.

Thank You, I love You. I am grateful.

Amen

Dear God,

Help me as I teach and share to convey my true passion and my genuine love for the people that I am teaching!

Help me to convey the real message that there is hope for a better way of living, a way out of the bondage of debt.

Help me to be as a light shining into darkness—the light of knowledge shining into the darkness of ignorance. This information is not made readily available, so people have to make an effort to seek knowledge and find answers.

If someone has done their part and made the effort to show up, help me to do my part, to understand the importance of helping others learn.

May my passion, belief and excitement shine through and be contagious as I share with others. Help me show them a way to freedom, abundance, purpose and well-being!

May my focus always be on helping others to realize their best possible life!

Thank You, I love You. I am so very grateful.

Amen

HUMILITY

"If my people, who are called by my name, will humble themselves and pray and seek my face and turn from their wicked ways, then I will hear from heaven, and I will forgive their sin and will heal their land."

—2 Chronicles 7:14

" 'Thank you' is the best prayer that anyone could say. I say that one a lot. Thank you expresses extreme gratitude, humility, understanding."

—Alice Walker

"It was pride that changed angels into devils; it is humility that makes men as angels."

—Saint Augustine

"Do you wish to rise? Begin by descending. You plan a tower that will pierce the clouds? Lay first the foundation of humility."

—Saint Augustine

"The Lord sends poverty and wealth; he humbles and he exalts."

—1 Samuel 2:7

"Your beginnings will seem humble, so prosperous will your future be."

—Job 8:7

Dear God,

Show me who needs to be blessed today, and how I can be an agent for You to provide that blessing.

Thank You, I love You. I am blessed. I am grateful.

Amen

Dear God,

Thank You for all the times I have been protected.

There are many times that I am completely aware of Your Divine intervention orchestrating events that otherwise could never have happened, and that kept me safe against all odds.

I'm positive that there are many more times when You and the Angels were working behind the scenes, protecting me in ways that I am completely unaware of, and I thank You for those times as well.

I trust that You are my ever present help in times of need, and my loving guide and protector. What a great confidence in all areas of my life, knowing that I am never alone, never without the One Who loves me the most!

Thank You, I love You, I am so very grateful.

Amen

Dear God,

Thank You for the health that I enjoy in this physical body!

To contemplate the enormity of all systems and cells working together in harmony is to be acutely aware of the miracle of life, and to believe in a loving intelligent creator. It can be no other way.

Thank You for a healthy body.

Thank You, I love You. I am blessed. I am grateful.

Amen

Dear God,

I come to You humbly, seeking Your loving forgiveness. There have been times that I've fallen short, and situations where I've chosen the wrong course of action, or caused someone pain (even if unintentional). There have been times that I wasn't the witness or example that I should have been for You.

I know it's all part of our human-ness and that everyone makes mistakes at times, but I ask that You please find it in Your omnipotence and grace to grant me the peace that comes from knowing that You have forgiven me.

By the same token, I forgive anyone who has caused me pain, or wronged me in any perceived way. I release "the story" and any negative emotions attached to it, as well as the need to be "made right."

I give forgiveness. I accept forgiveness.

Thank You, I love You, I am so very grateful.

Amen

INSPIRATION

"For I know the plans I have for you, declares the Lord, plans to prosper you and not to harm you, plans to give you hope and a future."

—Jeremiah 29:11

"I have not failed. I've just found 10,000 ways that don't work."

—Thomas Edison

"It's never too late to be what you might have been."

—George Eliot

"Everything you can imagine is real."

—Pablo Picasso

"I am enough of an artist to draw freely upon my imagination. Imagination is more important that knowledge. Knowledge is limited. Imagination encircles the world."

—Albert Einstein

"You have brains in your head. You have feet in your shoes. You can steer yourself any direction you choose. You're on your own. And you know what you know. And you are the one who'll decide where to go."

—Dr. Seuss

INSPIRATION

Dear God,

I believe that all inspiration comes from You!

I pray for inspiration for my next painting, for my writing, for teaching and helping others—help my work to be the very best that it can be, to help others bring out their very best!

Put love, joy, laughter, beauty, happiness, healing, radiance, peace, calm, and bliss into all my ideas and work(s). Inspire me!

Thank You, I love You. I am so very grateful.

Amen

Dear God,

Help me to be a light bearer, an educator, an encourager, an empowerer, a motivator, an inspiration, a way-shower, and a blessing to everyone in my life!

Help me awaken others, if only a little bit, to the great possibility and hope of living their very best lives each and every day.

Help me to live as that example (even on those days that aren't easy), and in such a way that I will hear You say, "Well done, good and faithful servant."

Thank You, I love You. I am grateful.

Amen

Dear God,

Let me live my life so that everything is filtered by what is good, and true and right, by what is of the most spiritual importance, by what most glorifies You, Lord!

Help me to be clear about the right thing at all times, to be aware of what actions will serve You and others, and to be an example of how to bring light in a world too full of darkness.

Empower me to make a significant positive difference in the lives of many, by whatever means You see fit.

Thank You, I love You. I am grateful Lord.

Amen

Dear God,

Thank You for Your loving care and guidance. Thank You for angels that watch over us throughout our lives: guiding, assisting and protecting us even when we are unaware.

Please help me to develop a greater sense of the spiritual aspects of this existence. I want to be able to sense, see, hear, and feel the presence of the angels who are here to help me. I want to be able to tune in and receive divine, pure and loving energies and guidance, so that my work—all of it!—will be truly inspired.

Thank You, I love You. I am blessed. I am grateful.

Amen

YOUR BEST FUTURE

"Commit your work to the Lord, and your plans will be established."

—Proverbs 16:3

"Trust in the Lord with all your heart and do not lean on your own understanding."

—Proverbs 3:5

"Destiny is not a matter of chance; It is a matter of choice. It is not a thing to be waited for; it is a thing to be achieved."

—William Jennings Bryan

"It is not in the stars to hold our destiny, but in ourselves."

—William Shakespeare

"You cannot connect the dots looking forward; you can only connect them looking backwards. So you have to trust that the dots will somehow connect in your future."

—Steve Jobs

"Let the future tell the truth and evaluate each one according to his work and accomplishments."

—Nikola Tesla

"Let us put our minds together and see what life we can make for our children."

—Sitting Bull

Dear God,

I pray for clear guidance and direction as I move forward on my life's path.

I have a tendency to become distracted or change course based on fear or worry ... so please help me stay focused, on course, determined and disciplined enough to see it through to completion.

Thank You, I love You. I am grateful.

Amen

Dear God,

My mind and heart are full of so many things I'd like to do! I need help focusing on one (or two) at a time.

Please help me discern which goals are most driven by love for others, based on solid, correct principles, and would be the most effective at helping people. Then help me sustain the motivation and the energy to complete those—to see them manifested into reality.

Let's co-create something amazing together, all with the goal of helping others by showing them a path to a more enlightened and empowered life.

Thank You, I love You. I am grateful.

Amen

Dear God,

Thank You that we can look into the future with hope, excitement and joy, resting in the assurance of Your loving guidance and Your desire to see us prosperous and empowered—as we seek to serve and help others.

Thank You, I love You. I am grateful.

Amen

Dear God,

Thank You for this amazing life, for the entirety of my journey here to this point. The lessons and the blessings, the people and the pets, my family and my friends. When I take time to really contemplate, I am amazed at the perfection by which each and every aspect is divinely guided, and how everything has been designed to bring me to exactly this point.

Such awareness brings great peace and comfort, as well as sincere gratitude. It is also a solid foundation for complete trust that You are overseeing the future as well. Who would dare to challenge the Creator of all things about His master plan for my life?

So, thank You for my life—all of it! And thank You for the assurance that the future is in Your hands as well. I am excited to see where we are going together!

Thank You, I love You. I am grateful.

Amen

Dear God,

Thank You for making it clear to me how You are using me to help so many people learn a better way—Your way!—of wellness.

I see the serendipities, the coincidences, and the unlikely "chance" meetings, where I just happened to meet someone who needed exactly what we have to offer!

Whether it be the natural support to their physical bodies through our amazing oils, our wonderful supplements, or maybe simply love and encouragement, it's such a blessing to be in a place to be able to help people get connected to answers to these needs!

For everyone who has a specific need—my family, friends, business associates, and acquaintances, and even those I've yet to meet—please bless them with Your love and goodness. Shower them with abundant health and well-being, so that Truth and Light and Love shall spread over Your beautiful Earth!

Make the world as it should be, as it was in the beginning, and as it will be again.

The world is re-awakening to the power of Love!

Thank You, I love You. I am grateful for everything You are.

Amen

Dear God,

There are so many demands on my time and for my attention. I pray for focus and clarity so that my energy and efforts are most effective.

I am truly grateful for the many wonderful people in my life, and I value each one of them. Help me to find a way to convey this in an honest, genuine, loving manner, and to be able to make the most of time spent with them.

One of my strong desires is to create freedom for myself, my family and friends—the people I love and care about. There are so many who are "stuck" and they are not even aware that there is an alternative. May I find the best, most loving way to show them that there is a way out, a path to freedom, a better way for them.

Give me the words, the materials, the time and the energy to bless everyone who wants (and those who need but don't understand yet!) to find their own best path—their own road to financial freedom and time freedom, and also to a much healthier lifestyle!

Bless me greatly Lord, so that I may have the freedom, the time and the resources to bless many!

Thank You, I love You. I am so very grateful.

Amen

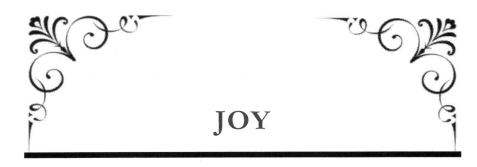

JOY

"But the fruit of the Spirit is love, joy, peace, forbearance, kindness, goodness, faithfulness."

—Galatians 5:22

"Now the God of hope fill you with all joy and peace in believing …"

—Romans 15:13

"Your success and happiness lies in you. Resolve to keep happy, and your joy and you shall form an invisible host against difficulties."

—Helen Keller

"It is the supreme art of the teacher to awaken joy in creative expression and knowledge."

—Albert Einstein

"Balance, peace and joy are the fruit of a successful life. It starts with recognizing your talents and finding ways to serve others by using them."

—Thomas Kinkade

"Joy is prayer; joy is strength; joy is love; joy is a net of love by which you can catch souls."

—Mother Teresa

"You make known to me the path of life; You will fill me with joy in Your presence, with eternal pleasures at your right hand."

—Psalms 16:11

Dear God,

This one is for my children and grandchildren. I pray that You bless them exceedingly with love, joy, peace, right work, a heart for You, and strength of character.

Help each of them to find their way to achieving their highest potential for You. I am blessed beyond measure for having them in my life.

Thank You, I love You, I am grateful beyond words.

Amen

*written 3-20-2015 (Spring Equinox + Solar Eclipse on the same day!)

Dear God,

Thank You for an abundance of joy in my life!

Life full of joy, all around: the sound of children laughing and playing, sunshine and music on a beautiful day, and feeling the joy of total oneness with Nature, with You, God, with everything—pure joy, my soul full with love for You, Your world, and everything in it!

Thank You for these joys that are part of everyday life ... life continually forging on!

What joy to be tuned in and appreciative of it all, and of my extraordinary place in this world. It's true that the more we focus on something, the more of it we find in our lives.

The one great joy of growing older is becoming aware of what is truly important. Help me get to the place where I can spend more time on these things and with these people, and let go of the unimportant things that consume my time. I am working on that just now.

As I create a more joy filled life, I can feel good knowing that I am showing others how to do the same!

Thank You for everything. You are everything. I love You, I am grateful.

Amen

Dear God,

Thank You for a life filled with wonder, with love, with joy and laughter!

Amazing gift, this life You have given me.

Let me use it well for You.

Thank You, I love You. I am Blessed. I am grateful.

Amen

Dear God,

Thank You for the gift of empathy and sympathy—for being able to know and understand what others are thinking and feeling.

This can be a gift when teaching, during mediation, and during negotiations at work.

At the same time, I sometimes "pick up" too much from others around me. Please protect me from any negativity, whether it be thoughts, words, feelings or situations. In other words, help me to be able to use my gift for helping others without personally "taking on" their problems.

Keep me full of positive life force, and surround me with Your love, Your grace and Your protection. Please keep Your divine love flowing through me and all around me, continually, so that I am free to comfortably be in the place of love, and feel the joy of being in service.

Thank You, I love You. I am so very grateful.

Amen

Dear God,

Thank You for the gift of joy! For the ability to reason and to understand and appreciate that life is full of joy—and is meant to be fully enjoyed! Some of the many things that truly bring me joy are:

Hearing my children laugh,

Watching the family grow,

Seeing my grandchildren smile, eyes wide with amazement,

Watching my fiancé's hands as he fixes things around house,

Enjoying a shower with clean, hot water,

Seeing a beautiful flower,

Eating delicious, pure, organic fruits and vegetables,

Spending time with family, friends and people we care about,

Smelling beautiful scents, such as Your plant essences,

Having someone's complete trust and confidence,

The smell of a newborn baby,

First steps, first words …

The love a pet can bring into a home,

The way pets adore us and depend upon us,

A beautiful home, nice vehicle,

Needs met,

Really connecting with someone, on a deep energetic, loving level,

Enjoying thunder and lightning from the safety of a comfortable bed,

Watching and listening to nature's power,

A sunny day with a cool breeze,

Walking on the beach,

Watching butterflies and birds,

A cool drink of water after working in the outdoor heat,

Money in the bank, and on hand, to enjoy,

Special occasions with the people we love: weddings, graduations, births,

Being valued,

Being heard,

Being understood,

Being loved,

Being appreciated,

A loving, wonderful family, and

Knowing that You love me and are helping me every step of the way!

I am Joy-ful! Thank You, I love You. I am so very grateful!

Amen

Dear God,

Thank You for the unmatched joy that comes from living in alignment with Your plan for my life, and for being an agent of Your love for many!

Thank You, I love You. I am grateful.

Amen

Dear God,

Thank You so much for the love, joy and happiness that our pets bring into our lives!

Thank You for the lessons they teach us—our beautiful, furry adorable examples of loyalty and unconditional love!

Help us to be worthy of their adoration, and provide them with the love and comfort that they deserve.

Thank You, I love You. I am so in awe and grateful.

Amen

PASSIONATE LIVING

"Whatever you do, work heartily, as for the Lord, and not for men."

—Colossians 3:23

"So whether you eat or drink, or whatever you do, do all to the glory of God."

—1 Corinthians 10:31

"My mission is life is not merely to survive, but to thrive; and to do so with some passion, some compassion, some humor and some style."

—Maya Angelou

"There is no passion to be found in playing small—in settling for life that is less than the one you are capable of living."

—Nelson Mandela

"Truly, truly I say to you, whoever believes in me will also do the works that I do; and greater works then these will he do."

—John 14:12

Dear God,

I desire most of all to live a life on purpose, with passion, accomplishing Your highest and best plan for me.

I ask that You make it abundantly clear exactly what that purpose is, and how I can go about achieving that goal.

I am passionate about helping others see their own true potential, and helping them begin their own journey through various paths to wellness and self-discovery.

If they need awakening, may I assist.

If they need encouragement, may I assist.

If they need inspiration, may I assist.

If they need motivation, may I assist.

If they need love and understanding, may I assist.

Please use me as the avenue to reach these searching souls, and give them hope. I am only the agent, or the broker, playing a small part in their own awakening as they open the door to their own personal journey.

Thank You for providing the desire to help, the means to do so, and the vision of how I can achieve this great purpose.

Please God, I myself need motivation, encouragement and help to bring this vision to fruition. May it be so, if it is Your will, God.

Thank You, I love You. I am grateful.

Amen

Dear God,

For all my adult life, when asked to ponder the question "Why am I here?" or "What is my purpose?" I would always immediately feel (or know) that the answer for me is to "Help Others."

Now, the question has become "How do I make a living while helping others?"

Thank You for guiding me to this place, this product, this company! I believe it is the answer to that question.

By focusing on that simple question: "How can I help?" and continuously developing myself through education, and growing personally as a leader, I know I can now take care of myself and those I love!

Thank You for Your wonderful, pure essential oils and for being part of a passionate, compassionate, faith based company that wants the best for all people.

I am honored to be part of their vision, and I pray Your continued blessings over me, over everyone in my organization, over all members, the company, and the founders.

I will be bold and ask for financial blessings as well, knowing that money in the hands of good people can do amazing things.

Magnify my purpose, and that of everyone on my team. Help us to help many others.

Thank You, I love You. I am blessed. I am grateful.

Amen

Dear God,

Help me live my best life now and always, filled with passion, love, joy and purpose. Bless my efforts to that end with Your favor, God.

Thank You, I love You. I am grateful.

Amen

Dear God,

I am truly grateful for my life, for all the wonderful people in my life, for the talents and ideas that You have given me, and for the determination and desire to see them through.

Thank You for the passion and the excitement I have about the work I am doing, for having developed certain skills over the years, for the ability to learn, share and teach, and for making me who I am and placing me on this most perfect path!

I am grateful Lord for the many blessings in my life; for beauty, joy, love and laughter, for empathy and compassion, for music, art, colors, wonderful scents, loving touches, kind words, and for family and friends that truly care and love one another unselfishly.

Thank You also for great food, for a beautiful place to live. Thank You that I have always been supplied ... and Lord, help me to get to a place where I can make a difference—a huge difference—in the lives of those who have known what it's like to be hungry, homeless, or helpless.

I am so aware of how truly blessed I am, and I sincerely desire to help many people, in many ways. Help me to know how to start making that significant difference. Help grow me into that person that has the skills, confidence, resources and knowledge to be a light to those in darkness, an encourager, a teacher, and an empowerer to the disheartened.

I am so very grateful, and want so much to help others … please add Your touch—Your divine favor and blessings—to my goals and plans, that many lives may be improved and many people uplifted to a better place, so that they can then help create a better life for people they know who need help, and on it goes!

Thank You, I love You. I am grateful.

Amen

Dear God,

Thank You for blessing me with intellect and understanding. As I seek to learn more about You and how I can become more like You, I am in awe at the power You have given us!

Lord, many have forgotten the teaching of Jesus that assures us that we have the power to achieve great things. Instead, we have come to accept great limitations as the norm.

Please clear me—my mind, body, spirit, subconscious and higher self, all of me—of all limiting beliefs and lower energies.

Please Lord, help me to train my focus on amazing abilities, empowerment, and ideas for loving service.

Use me as a conduit for Your loving energies, ideas, attributes, blessings to others, and positivity so that I can assist in raising up everyone I meet!

Protect me from any lower vibrations and make my work effective for You, God, for spreading love, light, and joy!

I'm so excited to watch what happens going forward in love, with You!

Thank You, I love You. I am blessed. I am grateful.

Amen

Dear God,

Thank you so much for the gift of a new day!

Too often we take for granted the fact that we are given our days, each one a new opportunity to do something for You, God.

May I make the best use of my time and my energy today, working with love and gentleness, kindness, enthusiasm, determination, persistence, and passion, toward the ultimate goal of helping many people on this planet, and hearing You say, "well done."

Help me to stay inspired and motivated, even in times where other things seem to pull me off course.

Help me to stay physically fit, my body remaining strong and my energy level high, so that my ideas can be brought into reality sooner rather than later.

I'm so excited and passionate about the work You have placed upon my heart, and I pray for Your continued guidance and direction in making it happen.

Thank You, I love You, I am so very grateful.

Amen

PURPOSEFUL LIVING

"Many are the plans in a man's heart, but it is the Lord's purpose that prevails."

—Proverbs 19:21

"The Lord will fulfill His purpose for me."

—Psalms 138:8

"And we know that for those who love God and are called to His purpose, all things work together for good."

—Romans 8:28

"The purpose of life is not to be happy. It is to be useful, to be honorable, to be compassionate, and have it make some difference that you have lived and lived well."

—Ralph Waldo Emerson

"Your purpose in life is to find your purpose and give your whole heart and soul to it."

—Buddha

Dear God,

You are love, and loving support to Your creation. Please send a beam of Your loving energy down to me, completely filling me, my body, every cell in my body, and the spaces between the cells in my body.

I choose You, God. I choose Love. Please guide and protect me, and direct my path. Let this body and this consciousness be of loving service to others, for You, always.

Thank You, I love You, I am ever grateful.

Amen

Dear God,

Thank you for a healthy physical body—my vehicle for doing the work You have for me to do on this plane.

We take for granted so much, not the least of which is our own health, well-being, and energy.

Please continue to keep me strong and fit, so that I can focus on creating the things You have placed in my heart to create!

Thank You, I love You. I am grateful.

Amen

Dear God,

Help me to remember that my work is actually a form of service and devotion to You, Lord.

With that in mind, help me to stay focused, steady and true, even when it would be easy to get frustrated and lose sight of the end goal.

How awesome it is to be able to truly care for others and set out with a genuine desire to help them improve their lives, in so many ways, and to be able to call that my "work!"

And that my work honors and serves You Lord, even better!

Thank You, I love You. I am blessed. I am grateful.

Amen

Dear God,

I envision a life whereby I am an agent of Your love. I see myself serving with love, by showing others how to create their own best life—full of joy, abundance, balance, love and harmony.

Help me to help those who want and need a better way of living, and are willing to do what it takes to make it happen.

I believe my role is that of a facilitator, helping open people's eyes and expand their awareness of what is possible, and for those who choose to take those important, self-empowering steps, to get them started with confidence and enthusiasm!

I cannot (nor do I want to) do their work for them. I want to be the one who helps them see the potential for changing their lives, and initiates the process with resources and support, but ultimately seeing them empowered and confident in leading their own charge.

Help me to be a testimony to everyone I know and everyone I meet that they do still have a choice, and can choose to build a life filled with love, joy, peace, contentment, laughter, and vibrant health!

Thank You, I love You. I am grateful.

Amen

Dear God,

It's so exciting to me that the more I read and study about angels, I'm learning that they want to help us achieve our life's purpose.

·In fact, it's part of their purpose to assist You in helping us!

I can think of several specific occasions where I truly believe angels protected me, and brought me specific and timely messages ... and I am so very grateful!

Please Lord, I am paying attention! I'm looking for signs—the coincidences and serendipities that I take as pointers that I am on the right path. Please make the way clear, and thank You for Your guidance and protection.

I am praying, seeking You, trusting, working, and waiting ...

Thank You, I love You. I am grateful.

Amen

Dear God,

My deepest desire is to live a life that You approve of, using my unique talents and abilities to help others and make the world a better place for everyone!

I have many ideas and plans along these lines, but Lord, it seems that worry and distraction keep me sidelined much of the time.

Becoming aware of this has been very helpful, as I can choose to stop these negative thoughts immediately and remove them as certainly as I would remove a pebble from my shoe, but awareness is only part of the solution.

Now I ask for Your help with clarity! Make the way clear, Lord! Make it clear to my understanding which course to take, and make the way clear before me, opening doors to providing the opportunities that clearly point me in the right direction. I'm ready. I believe!

Thank You, I love You, I am grateful.

Amen

MOTIVATION

"For with God, all things are possible."

—Luke 1:37

"Motivation is the art of getting people to do what you want them to do because they want to do it."

—Dwight Eisenhower

"Motivation will always beat mere talent."

—Norman R. Augustine

"Motivation is what gets you going. Habit is what keeps you going."

—Jim Ryun

"The way to get started is to quit talking and begin doing."

—Walt Disney

"When we are no longer able to change a situation, we are challenged to change ourselves."

—Viktor E. Frankl

"If you want to build a ship, don't drum up people to collect wood and don't assign them tasks and work, but rather teach them to long for the endless immensity of the sea."

—Antoine de Saint-Exupery

Dear God,

I am motivated ... to make a change in my life and the lives of many, to make a living at it, and to make a significant, positive difference in the world.

Please give me the inspiration and the guidance to make this a reality.

Thank You, I love You. I am grateful!

Amen

Dear God,

I pray for clear vision as I look to the future.

Give me indisputable evidence as I go about my days that I am on the right path (or if I am not, please show me clear guidance to get there).

I ask for wisdom and understanding, and then for motivation, and finally (and always) the energy to see it all through to an amazing and wildly successful finish—helping many people along the way in the process.

Thank You, I love You. I am so grateful.

Amen

Dear God,

I pray for my entire team,

That they find great meaning and purpose in sharing clean living,

That they meet the people who are searching for what we have to offer—people whose lives will be improved significantly,

That they are alert to the needs of others and aware of opportunities to lovingly offer a better way,

That they put forth the necessary effort to become knowledgeable,

That they become increasingly comfortable with and proficient at sharing with others,

That they understand the importance of being genuine and leading with love,

That they are motivated and inspired to share consistently, with many people, thereby not only helping those people, but increasing their own level of success and fulfillment at the same time,

That they understand the importance of consistent, gentle, loving follow up,

And especially that they are always grateful to You, God, for the amazing provision of essential oils!

Help each one to see that by helping others, and investing in their own health, they are creating an awesome future for many, many people, as well as for themselves!

I pray that everyone on my team truly thrives!

And the same for the company as a whole, for everyone who is part of the vision that it stands for!

Thank You, I love You. I am grateful.

Amen

Dear God,

So many times it seems my prayers are about how to be "on purpose," or about how to help others and live my life to the fullest.

Today I want to focus more on my physical body, which I probably take for granted too much of the time.

As my vehicle for navigating this world, help me to respect and appreciate it, and to realize the importance of keeping it in the best condition possible by choosing to implement good habits.

As the temple where Your Spirit dwells, even more so!

Only the best, cleanest, life-supporting food and drink should be tolerated. Activities that support strength and well-being should be part of my daily routine. I will keep this in mind as I go throughout the day and am faced with choices. Help me to remember that it's the consistency of small choices that add up to big returns!

I pray for Your loving hand on my physical body, for continued strength and good health, so that I have this body for a long, healthy lifetime of loving service Lord.

Heal whatever may need healing—at every level—down to every cell in my body and the energy and spaces between the cells!

Thank You, God, for a perfectly healthy body. I love You. I am grateful!

Amen

PEACE AND CALM

"And into whatsoever house ye enter, first say, peace be to this house."

—Luke 10:5

"For God is not the author of confusion, but of peace."

—1 Corinthians 14:33

"Better than a thousand hollow words, is one word that brings peace."

—Buddha

"Peace is a journey of a thousand miles and it must be taken one step at a time."

—Lyndon B. Johnson

"We can never attain peace in our outer world until we make peace with ourselves."

—Dalai Lama

"Peace begins with a smile."

—Mother Teresa

"Lord make me an instrument of Thy peace. Where there is hatred, let me sow love."

—Saint Francis of Assisi

Dear God,

Some days it seems like nothing goes smoothly and my patience is tested repeatedly.

Please assist me in maintaining my own peace within, regardless of any stress thrown my way.

I seek the perfect calm that comes from knowing that You are with me, and that is ultimately all that matters. And that You are more powerful than anyone or anything, and You have a perfect plan for my life that nothing can stop!

I thank You for that, and for whatever lessons are hidden in these seemingly backwards days. I trust You wholly, and am grateful for the peace that trusting in You provides.

Thank You, I love You. I am (even on these days, still) grateful.

Amen

PEACE AND CALM

Dear God,

Help me to keep my focus on You at all times, whether things are going smoothly or not, whether I am able to find quiet and peacefulness or not ...

Help me to always carry with me the awareness of You, and Your love that gives us that peace beyond understanding.

Seeking first You and Your continual presence within, I trust that all else can be safely surrendered and will work out. I trust Your plan God.

Thank You, I love You. I am grateful.

Amen

Dear God,

You are the Most High, the Absolute, the Diving Loving Creator of all!

You have taught us that we are Your children! And that as such, we are loved and provided for. This is so awesome—I can scarcely understand the reality and implications of this truth.

I am Your child, Your creation: valuable and worthy, provided for and protected, loved and cared for by You!

With the knowledge and understanding of this fact, there is absolutely no reason to worry or fret about anything!

I trust.

Thank You, I love You. I am grateful beyond words.

Amen

Dear God,

Thank You so much, God, for those (rare!) quiet times in my life! I don't mean to suggest that the "sounds of life" all around me are a negative … it's just that it seems like there are seldom times of complete silence and stillness.

And God, You said, "Be still and know that I am God." We need times of quiet and reflection, and it's becoming increasingly harder to find, it seems.

I appreciate the quiet and stillness, because it's during those times that I can "forget myself" and sense Your Divinity. It's then that I feel Your presence the strongest and can hear Your loving guidance.

So God, thank You for the quiet times, and help me to not be aggravated by the noises when it's not quiet. Help me to develop the ability to find that place of inner calm and connection, regardless of my environment or the level of activity around me.

Help me to hear Your voice above it all, and lead me to Your highest plan for my life.

Thank You, I love You. I am blessed, and so very grateful Lord.

Amen

PRESENT MOMENT

"Trust in the Lord with all your heart and lean not on your own understanding. In all your ways acknowledge Him, and He will direct your path."

—Proverbs 3:5–6

"To everything there is a season, and a time to every purpose under heaven."

—Ecclesiastes 3:1

"Do not dwell in the past, do not dream of the future, concentrate the mind on the present moment."

—Buddha

"You must live in the present, launch yourself on every wave, find your eternity in each moment."

—Henry David Thoreau

"Happiness is not something you postpone for the future; it is something you design for the present."

—Jim Rohn

Dear God,

Thank You for the gift of free will, and thank You for the assurance that You can and will bless our lives along the way, whichever choices we make.

Help me to realize that each moment has the potential to be a defining moment; I have the ability to choose at any instant which path I will take.

Guide, direct and protect me always, at each and every moment, as I seek to live in loving service to You.

Thank You, I love You. I am grateful.

Amen

Dear God,

I ask that You now and continuously help me to release subconscious ideas or beliefs that might be hindering me from moving forward in any way.

Take these fear based beliefs, transmute and transform them; replace them with Love based, empowering beliefs that will enable me to accomplish all the dreams that You have placed in my heart—my destiny!

May those who (unwittingly) gave me the old limiting beliefs (in an effort to protect me from pain, loss, or disappointment) see the change in me, realize my capacity for love, success, and amazing accomplishments, and support these as we all grow together on a higher path!

I am excited for an empowered and amazing future.

Thank You, I love You, I am so very grateful!

Amen

Dear God,

Help me to be careful not to use "acceptance of Your will" as an excuse to settle for less than Your perfect plan for me.

I accept where I am now, and all that has transpired in my life to this point, but that does not give me permission to stop moving forward and growing, learning and improving myself.

If I may, please help me find that healthy balance between contentment now and passionate, driven endeavors as I look to make a significant contribution to the world. Help me find happiness in the present moment, coupled with enthusiastic work now and into the future.

I am ever in awe, grateful, humbled. You are everything.

Thank You, I love You.

Amen

RELEASE

"I saw the angel in the marble and I carved until I set him free."

—Michelangelo

"You leave old habits behind by starting out with the thought 'I release the need for this in my life.' "

—Wayne Dyer

"There are really three parts to the creative process. First there is inspiration, then there is execution, and finally there is the release."

—Eddie Van Halen

"Creativity can release you from the limitations that the world has constructed around you."

—Robert LaSardo

"To get is simply to release, and then gently invite."

—Bryant McGill

RELEASE

Dear God,

I pray today especially for those who have experienced trauma and suffering in their life. I pray for their understanding that as victims of abuse, the fault was not their own, and that they do not have to "carry that story" as part of who they truly are.

Lord, You can heal the wounds. You can help them see a new life beyond the pain—perhaps even a life where they can help others who have suffered similarly.

Help them to re-frame these events from the past, and to be able to view them from the present as an experience they survived and learned from, an experience that has made them stronger than many people, and has given them a perspective of appreciation for all things good and true, and a hope for a bright and promising future.

If anyone carries guilt, help them to see that it is not only dis-empowering, but completely unnecessary, as Your grace and forgiveness is always available, and freely given to all who sincerely ask!

May they see each new day as a beautiful gift, and an opportunity to learn, grow and help someone who might be going through a similar trauma now.

Please love, guide and bless these precious souls. Help them to be set free for a new, abundant, happy healthy life! May I be available to help people in need and be a true blessing to them in their lives.

Thank You, I love You. I am so very blessed, and I am grateful.

Amen

Dear God,

Thank You for speaking to me through nature! Today was most amazing; I was able to observe simultaneously a lunar eclipse (on a pink full moon!) and a sunrise over the ocean.*

It felt very auspicious and significant. I feel it represents the closing of old paradigms that no longer serve me (or humanity), and the beginning of something amazing, bright, beautiful and beneficial to all!

I am ready and willing to release the old ways and I fully accept the new energies and blessings that are being issued in.

There is now joy in place of sorrow, abundance in place of lack, and ease in place of struggle. I am open to receiving the good that You are, that You freely give, and that You desire we have, so that we are better able to serve.

What a beautiful, unusual, amazing day! Thank You, God, Thank you, Angels for an awesome new beginning!

Thank You. I am ready to receive Your abundant blessings! I am grateful.

Amen

*April 4th, 2015: At 7:08 AM a lunar eclipse, at 7:11 AM a sunrise on the beach, on Easter weekend.

RELEASE

Dear God,

Please look deep into my heart, my thoughts and my beliefs, and give me clarity about what is true and real and valuable and important.

Help me to have clear discernment about situations and people in my life, and to make good decisions that support my spiritual advancement.

Help me be clear about what needs to be released, and empower me to achieve my very best for You, Lord.

My deepest desire is to do with excellence the tasks You have for me to do! Give me clarity, strength, and determination—daily—to make that my constant reality!

Thank You, I love You. I am grateful.

Amen

RELEASE

Dear God,

If there are limiting beliefs or blocks to my best life—my
highest potential for You, God, please help me release
them now, and for all time.

Free me from any negativity, known or sub-conscious.

Keep me focused and on purpose so that I achieve
what You have for me to do—my destiny!

Thank You, I love You. I am grateful.

Amen

Dear God,

Please hear my earnest prayer. Please assist me in releasing whatever may be limiting advancement toward my highest purpose.

Ideas, beliefs, habits ... whether conscious or unconscious, and no matter the origin, please be my constant guide and protector, my encourager, as I endeavor to examine these and let go of anything in the way of amazing success!

Help me to forgive anyone who may have given me these limiting beliefs. I am positive that their intention was not to limit me, but to protect me.

Help me forgive myself for time spent on many pursuits that clearly were not my highest and best use of time, but that I suppose had some value simply by being part of the path that brought me to the here and now. Every bit of what has made up my life has had a role in bringing me to this point, in who I am today, and the thoughts and beliefs I now espouse. By that token, I can simply choose to be in gratitude for everything that I have lived and learned through, and everyone who has been part of my life up to this time!

Now, with that perspective of everything having value and purpose, and moving me along my path, looking into the future becomes so very exciting!

I trust You. I trust Your plans and process for taking me where I need to be in my life. I ask that You help me to be keenly aware of the opportunities that are sent my way, and that I know beyond doubt what to do going forward, when to do it, and that many are served with love.

I'm so excited to see what tomorrow brings and how we work together to accomplish something truly wonderful!

I release. I forgive.

Thank You. I love You. I am grateful.

Amen

RELEASE

Dear God,

Please help me remove and permanently release any blocks that might be keeping me from my divine destiny.

Keep me in constant awareness of the love and support that You have promised. I pray that my Spiritual self and my Soul are always alert and guiding the physical self that is making its way through the world, so that every step is on the best path, and is a light for others to follow.

Thank You, I love You. I am grateful.

Amen

LIVING WITHOUT STRESS

"Peace I leave with you. My peace I give you … Do not let your hearts be troubled and do not be afraid."

—John 14:27

"The greatest weapon against stress is our ability to choose one thought over another."

—William James

"In times of great stress or adversity, it's always best to keep busy, to plow your anger and your energy into something positive."

—Lee Iococca

"Many of us feel stress and get overwhelmed not because we're taking on too much, but because we're taking on too little of what really strengthens us."

—Marcus Buckingham

"Do not be anxious about anything, but in everything, by prayer and petition, with thanksgiving, present your requests to God. And the peace of God which transcends all understanding will guard your hearts and your minds in Christ Jesus."

—Phillipians 4:6,7

"Now the Lord of Peace Himself give you peace always by all means. The Lord be with you."

—2 Thessalonians 3:16

Dear God,

I declare that today is the day that everything changes; I trust wholeheartedly that I am loved, supported and provided for, completely, so that there is no room in my life for worry, fear or distraction.

I declare that from now on I am living on purpose and passionately, with clarity of mind and excitement as I progress into the future, anticipating blessings— exceedingly, abundantly, above and beyond my wildest imagination!

Please Lord, bless this declaration and work along with me to see it through, day by day, hour by hour, minute by minute. These daily small successes will be honored and celebrated as important steps and building blocks toward the ultimate goal.

Thank You, I love You, I am grateful.

Amen

Dear God,

Thank You for the gift of sensitivity, for being acutely aware of energies around me, and for being able to read those energies and know the truth about people and situations, based on my soul's impression and the feelings I receive as a result of this inspired knowledge.

However, as a highly sensitive being, I ask for help in protecting me and my own energy from any negative influences. Love is the only presence welcome and the only power acting in my life, please.

Thank You, I love You. I am so very grateful.

Amen

Dear God,

I am seeking solitude and a quiet space, so that I can turn off the world and just meditate on You.

As I walk through these beautiful gardens, I try one alcove after another, one bench after another ... Each one quiet at first, but then there are always others coming along the path, their feet crunching the pebbles and the sound grating away at my attempts to find peace and quiet.

Then traffic, and (no!) the sounds of construction nearby, trucks rumbling, the incessant "Beep! Beep!" of equipment backing up, saws grinding ...

There are groups of children on field trips, laughing, talking, skipping along, as their teachers try to keep their focus on the flora and the lessons they have planned ...

There are golf carts rolling by leaving the odor of gasoline to overpower the delicate scents of the flowers. And—are you kidding me—a leaf blower?! I just want quiet!

Even in a place as beautiful and reverent as these botanical gardens, peace and calm elude.

What could be my lesson?

Embrace the laughter of the children (that one is easy).

Accept the world around me.

Go within—learn to be at peace within, regardless of outer circumstances.

Detach.

Release the need to control my surroundings.

Just Be.

Everything is as it should be.

Trust the process.

Breathe.

Relax.

Be at Peace.

I am blessed to be here. Many will never get the opportunity to experience a place as beautiful as this. I am grateful.

Thank You, I love You. I am still so very grateful.

Amen

SURRENDER

"Surrender yourself to the Lord, and wait patiently for Him."

—Psalms 37:7

"For as the heavens are higher that the earth, so are My ways higher than your ways, and My thoughts higher than your thoughts."

—Isaiah 55:9

"I have been driven many times upon my knees by the overwhelming conviction that I had nowhere else to go. My own wisdom and that of all about me seemed insufficient for that day."

—Abraham Lincoln

"Always say yes to the present moment. What could be more futile, more insane, than to create inner resistance to what already is? ... Surrender to what is. Say 'yes' to life and see how life suddenly starts working for you rather than against you."

—Eckhart Tolle

"Surrender your own poverty and acknowledge your nothingness to the Lord. Whether you understand it or not, God loves you, is present in you, lives in you, dwells in you, calls you, saves you and offers you an understanding and compassion which are like nothing you've ever found in a book or heard in a sermon."

—Thomas Merton

Dear God,

As much as I want to achieve something amazing, as much as I want to create something that will help everyone, and as much as I want to leave a great legacy by adding great value and leaving the world a significantly better place ... I totally surrender to Your will for my life.

There is only so much time in a day ... and so many days seem to be filled with things that can feel like "spinning my wheels," with what sometimes feel like small (dare I say insignificant?) things ...

Perhaps (could it be?), that Your best plan for my life is exactly this? To help in a myriad of small ways?

Although I don't understand why I would be given these great dreams and strong desires if it is not possible to attain them, if that is the way it is to be, then I will accept it.

Please make it known to me, in some way, so that I can be focused on doing the work I am to do. As long as it's Your plan, I trust completely and am more than willing to put forth every effort. I surrender to Your will completely.

Thank You, I love You. I am ever grateful.

Amen

Dear God,

I surrender to Your plan for my life; please make it immediately and obviously clear to me.

I have tried so many different things, and have done well, and made enough to get by, but still the magic that brings great success seems to elude me.

My plans, my efforts, my thoughts, my work at all these things ... I surrender to You. Put me where You want me, doing what You want me to do, please!

Or, perhaps this is it? My life as I am living it now, day by day in small acts of service?

Either way it's all Yours. It's all You.

Thank You, I love You. You are everything.

Amen

Dear God,

I put my total trust in You, confident and grateful that Your love and protection, guidance and direction are with me always.

Thank You, I love You. I am grateful.

Amen

Dear God,

At times when I feel like I am at a complete loss as to what to do in a certain situation, I trust that You are with me, that You already know the best outcome, and that You have everything under control.

Thank You, I love You. I am grateful.

Amen

TRANSFORMATION

"Do not be conformed to this world, but be transformed by the renewal of your mind."

—Romans 12:2

"Therefore if anyone is in Christ he is a new creature. The old has passed away; behold the new has come."

—2 Corinthians 5:17

"When she transformed into a butterfly, the caterpillars spoke to her not of beauty, but of her weirdness. They wanted her to change back into what she had been. But she had wings."

—Dean Jackson

"I tried to contain myself, but I escaped."

—Gary Paulsen

"Meditation is an essential travel partner on your journey of personal transformation. Meditation connects you with your soul, and the connection gives you access to your intuition, your heartfelt desires, your integrity, and the inspiration to create a life you love."

—Sarah McLean

"Chase love and joy as much as you can in each moment and watch your life transform."

—Amy Leigh Mercree

Dear God,

It says in Your word that "In the beginning was the Word, and the Word was with God, and the Word was God" (John 1:1). Science is now unveiling the same— that thoughts and spoken words actually have creative power!

Help us then to be ever mindful of our words and the creative power they contain.

May the words I speak to the people in my life be always loving, positive, empowering, encouraging, and transformative!

Please awaken each one of us to our own creative power through our thoughts and words, and help us to understand how vitally important it is to use positive, conscious language at all times.

Thank You, I love You. You are everything! I am grateful.

Amen

TRANSFORMATION

Dear God,

Help me to guard my thoughts, so that only what is good and pure and positive has the opportunity to take seed and grow in my life.

Thank You, I love You. I am grateful.

Amen

Dear God,

Thank You for Your love and forgiveness. Please help me to be more forgiving, of others, and of myself!

If You can see me in my best light and love me, I choose to be in agreement with that. And so it is.

Thank You, I love You. I am grateful.

Amen

Dear God,

Sometimes it's hard to rise above the daily grind—the pressures of work, busy schedules, demands and obligations, negative news, financial concerns … it can be so oppressive and disheartening.

Please awaken us to our true nature of love, connectedness, heirs to life infinitely abundant, and powerful to create any path aligned with Your highest purpose.

May I trust in the knowledge that You desire my prosperity and success, and may all my actions be bold, confident, and in agreement with Your desire for my life!

Thank You, I love You, I am grateful.

Amen

PART THREE

PRAYERS FOR YOUR PURPOSE
& YOUR BUSINESS

My Surrender

PRAYERS FOR YOUR PURPOSE & YOUR BUSINESS

Dear God,

Help me as I teach and share to convey my true passion, and my genuine love for the people that I am teaching!

Help me to convey the real message that there is hope for a better way of living, a way out of the bondage of debt.

Help me to be as a light shining into darkness—the light of knowledge shining into the darkness of ignorance. This information is not made readily available, so people have to make an effort to seek knowledge and find answers.

If someone has done their part and made the effort to attend a class, help me to do my part, to understand the importance of sharing, and to show up with excitement and be bold about helping others learn.

Otherwise they may never know what toxins and chemicals are doing to their bodies if not reined in!

Would I not readily offer a lifeline to a friend (or anyone!) who's drowning? This lifestyle is exactly that! A ticket to freedom, abundance, purpose and well-being!

May my passion, belief and excitement shine through and be contagious as I share with others.

May my focus always be on helping others to realize their best possible lives!

Thank You, I love You. I am so very grateful.

Amen

PRAYERS FOR YOUR PURPOSE & YOUR BUSINESS

Dear God,

I call upon You, Your infinite love and knowledge to guide my every step as I set out to achieve the dreams that You have placed in my heart.

I pray for clear focus and inspiration for exactly the correct thing, whether a collection of writings, new pieces of art, or sharing Your amazing oils as a natural way to support wellness ...

These are the things I love, the things I am passionate about, Lord. I truly believe in them, and I believe that the world needs them and will be better for having them! Please give me the inspiration in each and every moment, to know which to be working on—please INSPIRE beautiful, healing work.

In addition to inspiration, I ask for the motivation and focus to make it happen. With Godly inspiration, motivation, and passion, I believe that success is inevitable!

I am grateful for the talent, the passion and the drive that You have given me. You are indeed an awesome, loving Father who has provided me with everything I need. It is now up to me to put the dream into action! I pray that You bless my efforts and my work. Bless the people whose lives I touch through my teaching and work.

What a beautiful, inspired, joy filled way to live life! Where spirituality, creativity, work and love are all one and the same. That defines Heaven on earth!

Thank You, I love You. I am so very grateful!

Amen

PRAYERS FOR YOUR PURPOSE & YOUR BUSINESS

Dear God,

Thank You for Your amazing, wonderful world! Thank You for all of nature and the perfect harmony in Your loving, divine design. Thank You for the plants, and for all that they provide for us: food, clothing, shelter and more. And thank You for the gift of the essential oils of the plants; the life essence, the living intelligence and energy that they allow us to participate in!

Your world is nothing less than awesome God, and the more I learn, the more fascinated and "in awe" I am!

Lord, I want everyone to know and understand how amazing Your oils are. Please open their eyes and ears and hearts to the truth, so that they experience the wonders of nature's way.

Please use me as a messenger, helping those who need Your oils, and teaching people that they have a better, more natural way to be healthy.

Guide and direct my path, oh Lord. Put me where I need to be, and in contact with those who need (and want) this information!

I'm thrilled every time someone shares a success or transformation story—no matter how small—as they learn to experiment with and trust the gift of oils that You have given to us.

I'm honored to play a part in spreading this empowering and life changing information with Your world—one day at a time, one person at a time!

Thank You for each and every step of my life's path that has brought me to where I am at the present moment.

Thank You for hope and excitement for the future, and for finding "work" that has real meaning and purpose!

Thank You, I love You. I am blessed. I am grateful.

Amen

PRAYERS FOR YOUR PURPOSE & YOUR BUSINESS

Dear God,

For all my adult life, when asked to ponder the question "Why am I here?" or "What is my purpose?" I would always immediately feel (or know) that the answer for me is to "Help Others."

Now, the question has become "How do I make a living helping others?" Thank You for guiding me to this place, this product, this company! I believe it is the answer to that question.

By focusing on that simple question: "How can I help?" and continuously developing myself through education, and growing personally as a leader, I know I can now take care of myself and those I love!

Thank You for Your wonderful oils. Thank You this company's commitment to excellence and purity. Thank You for the lifelong study, the vision and determination that has made it the passionate, compassionate, faith based company that it is.

I am honored to be part of that vision, and I pray Your continued blessings over me, over everyone in my organization, over all members, and especially over our founders.

I will be bold and ask for financial blessings as well, knowing that money in the hands of good people can do amazing things.

Magnify my purpose, and that of everyone on my team. Help us to help many others.

Thank You, I love You. I am blessed. I am grateful.

Amen

PRAYERS FOR YOUR PURPOSE & YOUR BUSINESS

Dear God,

Thank You for providing all that we need for a healthy, happy, and prosperous life!

Your beautiful world is amazing God!

This life is full of gifts for those who can see.

Thank You, I love You. I am blessed. I am grateful.

Amen

PRAYERS FOR YOUR PURPOSE & YOUR BUSINESS

Dear God,

I pray for my entire team:

That they find great meaning and purpose in sharing clean living,

That they meet the people who are searching for what we have to offer—people whose lives will be improved significantly,

That they are alert to the needs of others and aware of opportunities to lovingly offer a better way,

That they put forth the necessary effort to become knowledgeable,

That they become increasingly comfortable with and proficient at sharing with others,

That they understand the importance of being genuine and leading with love,

That they are motivated and inspired to share consistently, with many people, thereby not only helping those people, but increasing their own level of success and fulfillment at the same time,

That they understand the importance of consistent, gentle, loving follow up,

And especially that they are always grateful to You, God, for the amazing provision of essential oils!

Help each one to see that by helping others, and investing in their own health, they are creating an awesome future for many, many people, as well as for themselves!

I pray that everyone on my team truly thrives!

And the same for our company as a whole, for everyone who is part of the vision it stands for!

Thank You, I love You. I am grateful.

Amen

PRAYERS FOR YOUR PURPOSE & YOUR BUSINESS

Dear God,

There are not words to adequately express how grateful I am for my life—the entirety of it—and all the blessings that You have given me.

It is from this place of sincere gratitude that I desire to give back to You—to live for You, Lord. My heart is pure in that desire, and my mind is clear ... I ask only that You make known to me what that highest calling would be, and show me how to attain that goal, even if it's one step at a time.

Enlighten me. Empower me. I am willing and ready to put the necessary work into bringing it about.

Motivate me. Inspire me. May there be no shortage of unique and wonderful ideas of ways to help people all around the world to improve their lives!

I feel I am being led to pursue all things having to do with healing and self-discovery, from the vantage point of energies ... Your beautiful provision for helping us live wonderful and wonder-filled lives, with multiple senses engaged.

I have a vision of a beautiful, fun, love-infused wellness center, shop and hangout ...

Please show me the path, the plan and the people needed and help me generate the resources to bring it to life!

Help me to show people how to overcome the current paradigm of being out of balance and depleted, and show them instead how to bring joy, balance, well-being, and happiness back into their lives.

Help me to help people connect to You, God, to source, to love, to return to the original AWE-some-ness that we were born with, and created to be!

Thank You, I love You. I am grateful.

Amen

PRAYERS FOR YOUR PURPOSE & YOUR BUSINESS

Dear God,

I envision a life whereby I am an agent of Your love. I see myself serving with love, by showing others how to create their own best life—full of joy, abundance, balance, love and harmony.

Help me to help those who want and need a better way of living, and are willing to do what it takes to make it happen.

I see my role as that of a facilitator; helping open people's eyes and expand their awareness of what is possible, and for those who choose to take those important, self-empowering steps, to get them started with confidence and enthusiasm!

I cannot (nor do I want to) do their work for them. I want to be the one who helps them see the potential for changing their lives, and initiates the process with resources and support, but ultimately seeing them empowered and confident in leading their own charge.

Help me to be a testimony to everyone I know and everyone I meet that they do still have a choice, and can choose to build a life filled with love, joy, peace, contentment, laughter, and vibrant health!

Thank You, I love You. I am grateful.

Amen

PRAYERS FOR YOUR PURPOSE & YOUR BUSINESS

Dear God,

Thank You for Your amazing, abundant world! For the many different life forms You created in both the plant and animal kingdoms. Even in the mineral world there is such diversity and beauty. And thank you that much of it can be beneficial to our health and well-being, and that this lost information is now coming back into our awareness.

How could anyone doubt a loving, divine, intelligent creative force when contemplating the magnitude of it all? Such balance and harmony is truly awe inspiring.

What a joy to be a part of it all!

May we all live in awareness and appreciation of how miraculous our very lives are, Lord, and therefore always be conscious of living on purpose and for You.

Thank You, I love You. I am so very grateful.

Amen

PRAYERS FOR YOUR PURPOSE & YOUR BUSINESS

Dear God,

Help me to be a light bearer, an educator, an encourager, an empowerer, a motivator, an inspiration, a way-shower, and a blessing to everyone in my life!

Help me awaken others, if only a little bit, to the great possibility and hope of living their very best lives each and every day.

Help me to live as that example (even on those days that aren't easy), and in such a way that I will hear You say, "Well done, good and faithful servant."

Thank You, I love You. I am grateful.

Amen

PRAYERS FOR YOUR PURPOSE & YOUR BUSINESS

Dear God,

Thank You that we can look into the future with hope, excitement and joy, resting in the assurance of Your loving guidance and Your desire to see us prosperous and empowered as we seek to serve and help others.

Thank You, I love You. I am grateful.

Amen

PRAYERS FOR YOUR PURPOSE & YOUR BUSINESS

Dear God,

As I am becoming more and more aware of subtle energies and how I am (greatly) affected by them, I ask for Your guidance and protection over me—body, mind, spirit, and energy field.

Help me see clearly what is beneficial to me, and what is not, and help me to implement any necessary changes in order to have the most sublime life now, and into the future!

Also, may I be a guide, showing others how to do the same, through my unique talents and abilities, and teaching about Your amazing essential oils.

Help me create and maintain an environment (at home and at work) that is conducive to peace, relaxation, joy, creativity, inspiration, love, happiness, and bliss here on Earth. Love, Love, Love.

Thank You, I love You. I am grateful.

Amen

PRAYERS FOR YOUR PURPOSE & YOUR BUSINESS

Dear God,

Today I ask that You honor the work that I do, and that many people are blessed by it.

You have taught us that it is Your desire that we live a full and abundant life. Help us to understand and fully realize what this means, and come into complete alignment with it, so that we can experience that which is our own best life!

Thank You for the people that I come into contact with, that You send my way Lord, and thank You for allowing me to be that vehicle by which they learn, grow and become empowered to live their own best life: spiritually, mentally, emotionally, physically, and even financially!

We desire first and foremost Your design for our lives, and want to be of loving service each and every day.

Thank You, I love You. I am so very grateful!

Amen

PRAYERS FOR YOUR PURPOSE & YOUR BUSINESS

Dear God,

Thank You for making it clear to me how you are using me to help so many people learn a better way—Your way!—of wellness.

I see the serendipities, the coincidences, and the unlikely "chance" meetings, where I just happened to meet someone who needed exactly what we have to offer!

Whether it be the natural support to their physical bodies through our amazing oils, our wonderful supplements, or maybe simply love and encouragement, it's such a blessing to be in a place to be able to help people get connected to answers to these needs!

For everyone who has a specific need—my family, friends, business associates, and acquaintances, and even those I've yet to meet—please bless them with Your love and goodness. Shower them with abundant health and well-being, so that Truth and Light and Love shall spread over Your beautiful earth!

Make the world as it should be, as it was in the beginning, and as it will be again.

The world is re-awakening to the power of Love!

Thank You, I love You. I am grateful for everything You are.

Amen

PRAYERS FOR YOUR PURPOSE & YOUR BUSINESS

Dear God,

Thank You for giving us the tools we need to assist in the elevation of the awareness of the people on this planet: teachers, books, videos, personal experiences and life lessons, dreams and visions, clean food and water, and our wonderful oils!

Our culture has been off track for too long, and I am so excited to be witnessing an awakening and a return to natural, pure, simple, honest ways of living.

I pray that more and more people learn, grow, and share what it means to live their best lives now.

May it please You to see people return to love and service, and to let go of the silly distractions that keep us from Your best design for our lives.

Let me be an instrument for You along these lines— teaching, guiding, awakening, and helping many!

Thank You, I love You. I am blessed. I am grateful.

Amen

PRAYERS FOR YOUR PURPOSE & YOUR BUSINESS

Dear God,

Help me to remember that my work is actually a form of service and devotion to You, Lord.

With that in mind, help me to stay focused, steady and true, even when it would be easy to get frustrated and lose sight of the end goal.

How awesome it is to be able to truly care for others and set out with a genuine desire to help them improve their lives, in so many ways, and to be able to call that my "work!"

And that my work honors and serves You Lord, even better!

Thank You, I love You. I am blessed. I am grateful.

Amen

PRAYERS FOR YOUR PURPOSE & YOUR BUSINESS

Dear God,

There are so many demands on my time and for my attention. I pray for focus and clarity so that my energy and efforts are most effective.

I am truly grateful for the many wonderful people in my life, and I value each one of them. Help me to find a way to convey this in an honest, genuine, loving manner, and to be able to make the most of time spent with them.

One of my strong desires is to create freedom for myself and the people I love and care about. There are so many who are "stuck" and they are not even aware that there is an alternative. May I find the best, most loving way to show them that there is a way out, a path to freedom, a better way for them.

Give me the words, the materials, the time and the energy to bless everyone who wants (and those who need but don't understand yet!) to find their own best path—their own road to financial freedom and time freedom—and also to a much healthier lifestyle!

Bless me greatly Lord, so that I may have the freedom, the time and the resources to bless many!

Thank You, I love You. I am so very grateful.

Amen

PRAYERS FOR YOUR PURPOSE & YOUR BUSINESS

Dear God,

Show me who needs to be blessed today, and how I can be an agent for You to provide that blessing.

Thank You, I love You. I am blessed. I am grateful.

Amen

PRAYERS FOR YOUR PURPOSE & YOUR BUSINESS

Dear God,

Thank you so much for the gift of a new day!

Too often we take for granted the fact that we are given our days, each one a new opportunity to do something for You, God.

May I make the best use of my time and my energy today, working with love and gentleness, kindness, enthusiasm, determination, persistence, and passion, toward the ultimate goal of helping many people on this planet, and hearing You say, "well done."

Help me to stay inspired and motivated, even in times where other things seem to pull me off course.

Help me to stay physically fit; my body remaining strong and my energy level high, so that my ideas can be brought into reality sooner rather than later.

I'm so excited and passionate about the work You have placed upon my heart, and I pray for Your continued guidance and direction in making it happen.

Thank You, I love You, I am so very grateful.

Amen

PRAYERS FOR YOUR PURPOSE & YOUR BUSINESS

Dear God,

I thank You for a truly amazing team of people that share my vision and the goal of helping many find a better, more natural lifestyle with Your pure essential oils.

I know that You have sent each one into my life, for me to bless, and to be blessed by them. Thank You for their respect and their trust as they share their stories and their needs with me. I love every one of them—they each mean so very much to me.

I pray that You bless our entire team, Lord, each and every one, with blessings so amazing that there can be no doubt that it was because of You; so AWE-some that everyone will know that they could not have done it without Divine help.

I pray that each one sees their lives altered in a profound and positive way, so that they are free to help others even more.

I pray Your blessings and Your hand of favor over each person on my team, on all of us, Lord.

For freedom from the very real bondage of debt.

For freedom from the job that has become a tiresome grind.

For freedom from the job that lacks meaning or purpose.

For freedom from feeling stuck, and seeing no way out.

Lord, every single person that I know on my team has a wonderful, loving heart, and they want first and foremost to help others. They are so loving and nurturing, and many of them have a hard time believing that it's OK for them to be on the receiving end of love and blessings!

Please Lord, these are wonderful, giving people, and they all truly deserve to be blessed.

We have all worked hard.

We have all continued to give of ourselves, even when it's difficult to do so.

We have all given our money to help others, even when it was not easy.

We have all held on to hope.

We have all been nurturers, pouring into others, even ahead of ourselves.

We have all remained faithful.

We have all struggled long enough, Lord.

It's time to bless these dear souls. I want to pray for each one by name, and I pray that You see each and every one, see their situations. I pray You see that these are people that, if given time freedom and financial freedom, will use it well to continue to bless others further. They are the people that, if given the option and the means, will make a significant, positive difference in the world.

I know that with Your love, Your blessings, and Your favor, this team of amazing people will be able to do great things and help many! I love and appreciate them, every one.

I pray that You see it so.

Thank You, I love You. I am eternally grateful.

Amen

Dear God,

I love how full my life is!

I do truly enjoy being there for the people I love: my family and friends and my business associates. And I want to be always available and supportive to them all. But sometimes it can become overwhelming. It can seem like everything and everyone else takes priority, leaving me tired and drained—physically, mentally and emotionally, even spiritually.

Please help me to find a way to accomplish all that needs to be done, and to be that loving support to those I love, while taking great care of myself with proper nutrition, rest, exercise and the luxury of options for enjoying free time.

Lord I need time for my own creativity; to paint, to write, to just enjoy the beach, and to read. And I need time to "just be" with my family, and my closest friends.

I know that in order to help others, I have to first be in a strong place myself. I ask You to help me keep this understanding in mind as I learn to manage my time and energy (especially as my wonderful team continues to grow).

Thank you, I love You. I am so very grateful!

Amen

PART FOUR

HOW TO BE SURE YOUR OILS ARE PURE

Natural Healing

How to Know
You Are Using the Purest
Essential Oils Available

Perhaps you have heard, "Well, all essential oil companies say the same thing, so …"

This is equivalent to saying that you don't care enough to dig in and do enough research to be certain that you are only using the best, purest essential oils on your body and in your home.

If you are making the effort to rid your life of chemicals by choosing to use all natural products, then why in the world would it be acceptable to use an oil that contains anything other than the pure essential oil, as it was in nature with the constituents completely intact, with nothing added, and nothing taken away?

If you are going to expose your body to essential oils in any way—whether applying topically, ingesting, or simply inhaling them—you must make sure that you are not inadvertently right back where you started: unknowingly introducing toxins into your body.

If you are serious about cleaner living and using essential oils as part of your new lifestyle, there are some things you need to know.

Everything matters when you are using essential oils to support a healthy body. Everything!

In the process of producing essential oils, if anything at all is changed, or is "off," then the entire composition is changed. While it may still smell like lavender or peppermint, it will be devoid of the living energy and constituents that make it effective.

There are so many factors that go into producing truly pure essential oils. Here are some questions you should always ask any company, so you can be sure:

Does the company own their own farms? Or do they buy oils from another source and just put their label on the bottle?

Is the land clean? Is only purified water used for irrigation?

Are pesticides used on the plants? Or do they hand weed?

Is there a team of scientists and pharmacists on staff?

Do they test for peak potency every hour, and then every fifteen minutes before harvesting?

Do they know that some plants are more potent if harvested in early morning, and others if harvested at different times of the day?

Do they know which plants are best distilled immediately after harvest, and which will be more effective if left to "rest" for a certain period of time before going into the distillery?

Do they own or build their own distillery on the farms, so that the plant material doesn't lose potency while traveling?

Do they have volumes of data from decades of research done on every single batch that shows the exact best time, temperature and pressure for each plant? (And yes, each plant has its own "preference" for these factors, in order for its constituents to remain intact and effective.)

Are the distillers topped with a cone or a dome? (Do they even know why this matters?)

Can anyone tour the farm and the distillery, and talk to any of the employees, at any time?

Do the oils come into contact with aluminum or plastic, or only glass and stainless steel throughout the entire process?

Have they dedicated a lifetime to the study of essential oils? Or are they "newly on board" because of the recent surge in popularity?

Is every single batch quality tested in house, by many scientific tests?

Is every single batch also quality tested by third-party labs, as an extra measure of certainty?

How many oils and oil blends do they offer?

How long have they been in business?

Etc.

Asking these questions quickly reveals which essential oils can be trusted as truly pure!   (Hint: it's less than 2% of all essential oils produced for consumer use.)

Did you have any idea that so much went into producing pure oils for our benefit?

Sadly, I would venture to say that many essential oil companies themselves might not even know or understand that there is so much more to it than extracting the oil from the plant.

If you are buying oils at a farmer's market or a health food store, and the label says "pure," you must still do extensive research before trusting these oils on (or in!) your body. Did you know that the FDA will allow a label to say "pure" with as little as five to ten percent pure oils?

What if the bottle says 100 percent pure? Well, we still need to find out if they have come into contact with pesticides, plastics, aluminums, or other solvents or chemicals commonly used to extract oils in other companies.

What if they say 100 percent pure, and organic? Then we still need to know at what temperature they were distilled, and for how long, and at what pressure. Because if any one of these is "off," then you have just purchased nothing more than a scent. The constituents will not all be present and therefore the efficacy will be compromised.

Perhaps you had no idea before reading this chapter that there was such a huge difference in essential oil quality (and in the companies that produce them). Now you can understand something of just how much goes into producing completely pure essential oils. And you can see why it's important to have this knowledge if you are choosing to use oils to support your well-being. Anything you put on—or in—your body, anything you inhale, you want to be absolutely clean and pure.

PART FIVE

FURTHER IMPORTANT INFORMATION

Vibrant Inner Light

THE BASICS OF USING
ESSENTIAL OILS

You can find many books on the safe and effective use of essential oils to support wellness, however, thinking about the continuum, whereby there might be someone reading this book who has little knowledge of how to use essential oils safely, we must cover the fundamentals.

There are three main schools of thought when it comes to using essential oils, which leads to three methods of application: inhalation, topical application, and ingestion. [3]

To enjoy oils you can simply open the bottle and inhale the aroma, as the molecules are, in fact, still making their way into your system. You might like to let one drop fall into the palm of your hand, rub your hands together, and then cup your hands over your nose and mouth to inhale directly. And, of course, a (cold steam!) diffuser is another great way to get the benefit of the essential oils by breathing them in. I love to diffuse my favorite oils, because then everyone in the house receives the benefits!

---

[3] !! It is of utmost importance that you only ingest pure essential oils that are labeled for ingestion. Even if others claim to be 'pure', do not ingest. The FDA allows a label to say 'pure' with as little as five to ten percent pure essential oil. If anything at all is added, it will not only alter the compounds (therefore reducing effectiveness), but it could also be toxic. This brings up a good question: since our skin is our largest organ, and it literally takes in what we apply topically, how is it safe to topically apply an oil that is labeled "not for internal use"? Think about it.

Applying oils topically is another way to enjoy your essential oils, as the oils literally absorb into your skin, and disperse into the cells of your body.

Some oils are fine to apply "neat" (without dilution), while some of the "hotter" oils might be best diluted with organic coconut oil, especially if you are just starting out with pure essential oils, which are very potent. Everyone is different, so make sure you respect the power of the oils and start slowly with topical use.

To use oils topically, you could let a drop fall into the palm of your hand, rub your palms together, and then apply to the desired area. See the next section with the precautions, please! There are areas of the body that you do not want to put oils directly onto, among a few other cautions to be aware of. So, do not skip that section … Promise.

One of the best—and safest—ways to apply the oils is to the bottom of your feet; the skin is usually not as sensitive there, yet at the same time, the oils can quickly absorb into the cells of your body.

There is only one essential oil company to my knowledge that has created a line of oils with labeling specifically for ingestion. I cannot emphasize enough that you should never ingest any other oils. Without the strictest of guidelines and testing, you are never sure if you might be ingesting solvents, pesticides, sweeteners, extenders, or fillers, all of which will not only alter the original properties, but are likely toxic to the body.

If you have the purest oils, labeled for ingestion, one idea for ingesting them might be to place one drop in a glass of water, or add to your protein shake or smoothie. (Do not use containers made of plastic or Styrofoam.)

The oils safe for ingestion can also be used in recipes! Remember that they are very potent, so it does not take much at all. Sometimes even one drop can overpower a recipe, so to get a half drop, just insert a wooden toothpick into the top of the bottle and then stir into your recipe.

Whether you intend to Inhale, Apply Topically, or Ingest your oils, please see the list of precautions to be observed with even the purest essential oils.

Don't be nervous; we all started at the same place. Just get educated, make sure you are using only the purest essential oils, use common sense, and ENJOY the journey!

Make sure to get a trusted reference guide. That is the single best resource you can have for the practical and safe use of essential oils. My personal favorite is the "Essential Oils Desk Reference" by Life Science Publishers.

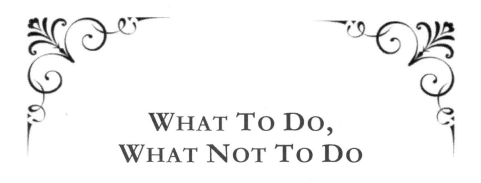

What To Do, What Not To Do

As mentioned, there are some general guidelines and precautions to be aware of, even if you are using the purest of essential oils.

Test an area of the skin to make sure you won't react to the oils. If you do feel uncomfortable, do not rinse with water. Instead, cut the oil with an organic coconut oil or olive oil.

Keep away from children.

Keep in a cool place out of direct sunlight.

Do not put oils with menthol, such as Peppermint, on the neck of a child under two and one half years of age.

If applying citrus oils, avoid the sunlight for seventy-two hours. If you want to apply a citrus oil, just apply where the sunlight won't hit, such as the bottom of the feet.

Do not put oils into your eyes or ears. If oils get in your eyes, sooth with organic vegetable oil, not water.

Wash hands thoroughly before handling contact lenses.

If you have any medical condition consult your Doctor or Naturopath about using oils.

If you are pregnant or nursing, consult your health care provider about using oils.

If you want to add oils to your bath, put Epsom salt first to help disperse the oils.

Dilute oils you take internally with an oil soluble liquid such as honey or coconut milk.

Only ingest pure oils specifically labeled for ingestion.

** You are encouraged to further your study of essential oils independently. **

How to Study Properties of Essential Oils Blends

My favorite reference for studying the many possible benefits is full of information about each of the oils: its place of origin, the breakdown of its constituents, how that oil was used historically, and the properties that it is known for. Additionally, if that oil was mentioned in the Bible, the scripture reference is given. To research an individual oil, you would look up the name of each plant in the section on "Single" oils.

If you want to know what you might expect from a Blend of oils, start by looking up each of the single oils that make up that blend.

The following are some examples of what you might find:

Rose: elevates the mind, creates a sense of well-being, may help overcome insecurities, and much more …

Bergamot: calming, mood uplifting, and much more …

Ylang Ylang: enhances spiritual attunement, may combat low self-esteem, focuses thoughts, and more …

Lemon: may increase mental accuracy, invigorating, clarity of thought and purpose, and more …

Geranium: may help release negative memories, may ease occasional nervous tension, lifts the spirits, and more …

Jasmine: beautiful, seductive fragrance, may counteract hopelessness, and more …

Palmarosa: may promote feelings of security, may support healthy digestion, may reduce feelings of occasional stress, and more ...

Roman Chamomile: calming, may help dispel anger or release emotions linked to the past, and more ...

Rosewood: empowering, may help stabilize emotions, and more ...

Melissa: calming, uplifting, may help balance emotions, may promote a positive outlook on life, and more ...

Helichrysum: uplifting to subconscious, and much, much more ...

Angelica: may release negative feelings, relaxing, may restore memory to before trauma, and more ...

Frankincense: stimulates the mind, elevates the mind, spiritually uplifting, and much more ...

Sandalwood: may enhance restful sleep, grounding, stabilizing, may help clear cellular memory, and more ...

Lavender: relaxing, calming, may reduce mental stress, and more ...

Neroli: may stabilize emotions, uplifting, inspiring, peaceful, sensuality, may encourage confidence, and more ...

Spruce: believed to carry the frequency of prosperity, may clear emotions, may increase sense of balance, and more ...

Blue Tansy: relaxant, and more ...

Juniper: may elevate spiritual awareness, love, peace, and more ...

Anise: may open emotional blocks, may recharge energies, and more ...

Tangerine: calming, may promote happiness, balance emotions, and more ...

Black Pepper: empowering, energizing, may stimulate metabolism, and more …

Orange: joy, peace, happiness, security, may clarify thoughts, and more …

Hyssop: may stimulate creativity, may support meditation, and much more …

Spanish Sage: may support healthy digestion, soothing, and much more …

Important Note: The reason for ending each list with "and more …" is so that this resource remains compliant. This means that I have intentionally chosen to leave out any benefits that have to do with the physical body, or any specific medical condition. Please refer to your trusted reference for a more exhaustive list of benefits for each of the specific oils.

This partial list of single oils can give you an idea of which pure essential oils you might like to use in combination with a particular prayer.

Again, there is so much more that you can learn with further study.

Enjoy the journey!

Final Notes/Further Study

References: **

"The Holy Bible," King James and other versions

"Healing Oils of the Bible" by David Stewart, Ph.D.

"Essential Oils Desk Reference" by Life Science Publishers

****

Connect on Facebook: "Janine Wooten"

"Praying in the Power Zone with Pure Essential Oils,"

"Best Life Practices," and

"Healthy with Oils"

****

Have you always wanted to publish your own book? I learned everything I needed to make it happen here:

https://tinyurl.com/yac7robk

****

** You are encouraged to do your own research; there are many trusted resources available. It's very important to pray for guidance and discernment when investigating essential oils.

****

Thank you for your interest in this book. I pray that you are blessed as you recite the prayers and apply pure essential oils during your prayers. Please, if you enjoyed it, leave a review on Amazon.com so that others can find it and be blessed as well. May God Bless You!

~ Janine L Wooten

****

If you would like to know which oils I personally love and use with these prayers please email AuthorJanineWooten@gmail.com to request a free companion guide to this book. Please use a clear Subject line such as "Requesting Companion Guide", so I see it. ☺

4 The information contained in this book is for educational, entertainment and enlightenment purposes only. It is in no way intended to diagnose, treat or claim to cure any medical condition. This information should not be used in place of qualified medical advice. The purpose of this book is to help the reader achieve a more powerful and connected prayer experience.

ACKNOWLEDGMENTS

There are so many people to acknowledge, it's literally impossible to name each individually. I realized when starting to write this section that I am so very blessed; every person in my life has been positive, encouraging, celebrating successes alongside me, and just the most loving people I can imagine. How many people can honestly say that? So, if you are in my life, thank you for your contribution to making it the amazing journey that it is. I love and appreciate you.

Thank you to my fiancé Johnny, for always believing in me, and showing me nothing but love, support and encouragement, even when (especially when!) others were telling me to "get a real job." Thank you for accepting and appreciating who I am and pushing me to follow my heart. I love you.

Thank you to Chip, Mark and Sean for always being loving and respectful, and for becoming young men that we are so very proud of; strong men with a heart for God, who are loving and respectful to your wife/girlfriends and families, who have a strong work ethic, and a desire to help others and always do what is right. And to Lindsey, Taylor and Tiffany, for being amazing young women, loving them, and helping make them the men they are. I hope this book makes you as proud of me as I am of you, and shows you all that you can do anything that you set your heart and mind to. Go after your best lives! I love you all.

Thank you to my mom and dad, for bringing me here! Thank you for your constant and faithful love, for always being there, for your encouragement, for believing in me, and for being amazing teachers and role models. I would not be who I am without you. I love you.

Thank you to all my siblings (especially Ann, who shares my love for essential oils and understands the passion behind this project) and my "life-long" friends for always being there, for being my sounding board, for always "having my back", and for your constant love, encouragement and support, even knowing the not-so-perfect parts of me better than most. I love you all.

Thank you to my "oily" family/new friends who inspire me to continually learn and grow into a leader worthy of your following. I know that first and foremost each one of you has a heart for helping others, and I pray that you are blessed with a beautiful life of doing so. I appreciate having each one of you in my life. I love getting to know you and watching you grow. I love you.

Thank you to the leaders in essential oil purity, for dedicating a lifetime to the study and production of pure essential oils. Thank you for being faithful – good stewards of God's precious provision. Your passion and your heart for helping is unparalleled; you are such an inspiration. You are both amazing. You are appreciated. You are loved.

Thank you to Mrs. Williams, one of many good English teachers, who taught me how to write and the importance of good writing. Even though you thought I was cutting up and not listening... Look at me now! Thank you.

Thank you to Chandler Bolt, Sean Sumner, Kandi Johnson, Ramy Vance, Spencer Borup, Sushmitha Naroor, and Jyotsna Ramachandran, and the entire SPS community, without whom this book would still be a private collection of words in a journal. Thank you for your patience and guidance throughout the publishing process. I appreciate you all.

And, a special shout out to Kaya, our 15-year-old Rottweiler mix, rescue dog, who was at my side - literally either beside me or under my desk, keeping my feet warm - throughout the entire process. What an amazing example of unconditional love and companionship. If I can be half as good as you... I love you.

And most importantly, I want to Thank God! For making me who I am, and for placing the desire in my heart, and giving me the talents necessary to make it happen. I love my life. Thank You. I am grateful beyond words. I love You!

****

The images in this book are original creations painted by the author, Janine Logue Wooten. You can learn more at MandalaGallery.com.

If you found value in "Praying in the Power Zone" please leave a review so that others can find it as well:
https://tinyurl.com/y82mgccn

Made in the USA
Columbia, SC
25 March 2018